RAILWAY · TIMES ·

Contents

The · Transport · Treasury

TIMES SERIES

Front Cover: Stephen Townroe's classic original colour view of No. 36001 at Eastleigh just prior to official inspection in June 1949. Number decals etc. have yet to be added whilst some cleaning has been undertaken on the roof line – note the man on the ladder has a paint pot in hand. This may be an appropriate time to refer to a conversation at Brighton between Gordon Nicholson the SR Motive Power Superintendent and Granshaw the Brighton Works Manager. When Nicholson asked, 'How are you going to balance the offset boiler?' The reply from Granshaw was, '...that is a good question, we are still trying to find the answer'. *S C Townroe*

Above: When life ran at a slower pace.....Collett 22XX 0-6-0 No. 2221 with a rake of three coaches in the new standard livery which soon came to be known as 'blood and custard' gets some admiring glances from two small girls, the daughters of the photographer, perched on a bridge parapet between Whitchurch (Town) and Sutton Scotney on the DN&S route. *S C Townroe*

Rear Cover: Branch line closures continued at a leisurely pace in the late 1940s and here Reid Class C16 4-4-2T No. 67496 is seen at Haddington on an unrecorded date in 1949 having received its new numbering and 'British Railways' lettering in January of that year. The branch from Longniddry on the ECML to this royal burgh and county town of East Lothian closed from 5 December 1949. *NS 206000A*

Copies of many of the images within **RAILWAY TIMES** are available for purchase / download.
Wherever possible illustrative material has been chosen dating from 1949 or is used to reflect the content described.

In addition the Transport Treasury Archive contains tens of thousands of other UK, Irish
and some European railway photographs.

© Jeffery Grayer. Images (unless credited otherwise) and design The Transport Treasury 2023

ISBN 978-1-913251-56-7

First Published in 2023 by Transport Treasury Publishing Ltd.,
16 Highworth Close, High Wycombe, HP13 7PJ

www.ttpublishing.co.uk or for editorial issues and contributions email to **admin@ttpublishing.com**

Printed in the Malta by the Gutenberg Press.

Introduction

Welcome to this second issue of 'Railway Times' covering 1949 and forming part of the 'Times' stable of Transport Treasury magazines recently enhanced by an 'Eastern' volume. Following the premise laid out in RT1 we attempt once again to fit as much as possible within the 80 pages whilst examining some of the developments, ranging from the significant to the bizarre, that the year 1949 heralded. This year saw the retirement of three of the great locomotive engineers Hawksworth, Peppercorn and Bulleid all of whom certainly left their mark on the railways of Britain although perhaps not always in the form of a lasting legacy; as was the case with the never to be repeated Double Deck EMU experiment, the short lived Tavern Cars and the perhaps best forgotten Leader fiasco. Branch line closures rumbled on although at nothing like the pace of later years and several old stagers on the locomotive front were steamed for the final time.

Exciting new developments encompassed the electrification of not only the Liverpool Street – Shenfield service but the introduction of electric locomotives on the Newhaven boat trains. New locomotives continued to roll off the production lines with two new classes of pannier tank being introduced together with a new diesel shunter for the Southern Region. The formation of British Transport Films played a large part in bringing developments in public transport, covering not just railways but roads and canals, to the attention of the general public and indeed such was the quality of some of the films produced in later years that they garnered many awards.

Elements of the expected standardisation following the formation of a nationalised industry are covered in further details of liveries to be adopted and in the proposed standard cab layout for the new classes of steam locomotive. Safety improvements always of paramount importance, are to the fore in the construction of new all steel coaches and thankfully as witnessed in the drastic reduction in the number of fatalities, 60 of which were recorded the previous year, but nil for 1949. However, this does not mask a very high level of death and injuries amongst railway staff that would surely be completely unacceptable today.

The lighter side of things is not forgotten with mention of pigeon specials, buffet car and refreshment room prices, station gardens competitions, BR's own model railway and how the industry attempted to woo prospective employees by way of a special booklet 'British Railways Welcomes You' featuring a series of somewhat quirky, and to our eyes, patronising cartoons. Once again many illustrations from the extensive Transport Treasury archive have been included to amplify the written word.

Finally, it is sobering to look at the route map produced by BR in 1949 and featuring in the centrefold of this issue which reveals the staggering loss of routes that has been experienced over the last 75 years. I hope you find something of interest in this issue and keep your eyes out for No. 3 covering 1950 which will be published in the spring of 2024. Once again any comments or contributions for future numbers would be welcomed.

Editor: Jeffery Grayer

The complete rake of carriages in the striking new livery, more properly called crimson lake and cream, enhances this view of A1 No 60159 *Bonnie Dundee* passing Aberlady Junction (for the short branch to Gullane) with the Up 'Heart of Midlothian' working. The curved train nameboard might just be seen above the front framing. No 60159 entered service from Doncaster Works on 24 November 1949, although the named train did not start operating until 1951 running between Kings Cross and Edinburgh. This particular image was taken in 1954. So popular were these named trains with the public that a thriving business grew up producing postcards of this and other named services.
S C Townroe

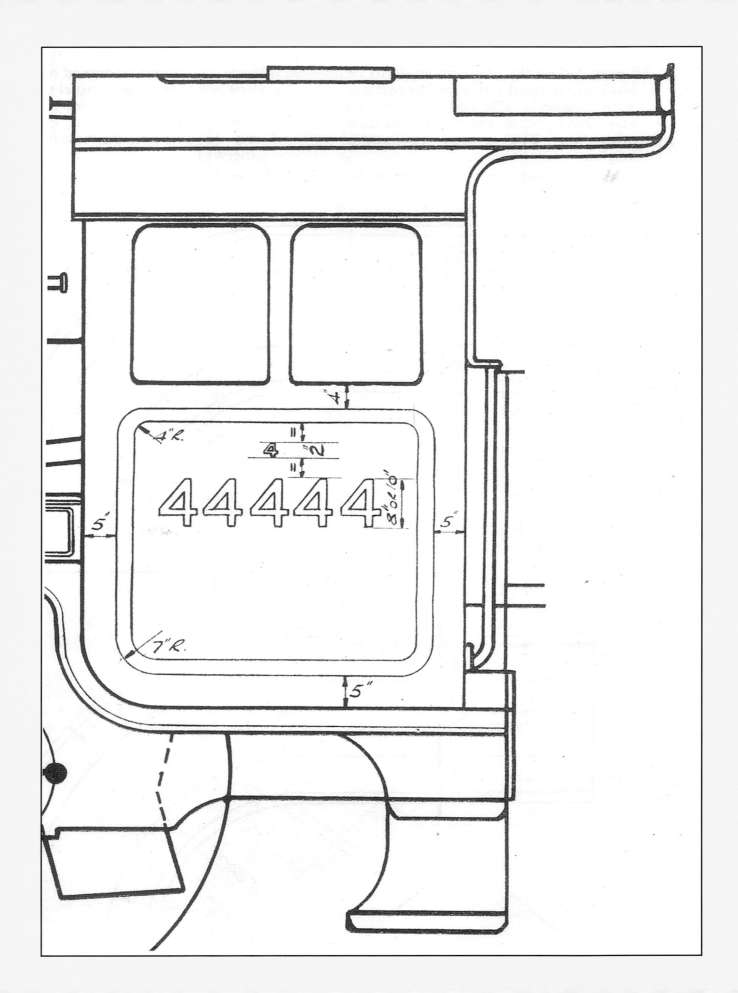

BR Standard Liveries

ollowing last year's extensive consultation exercises with locomotives and rolling stock being exhibited in a variety of colour schemes BR has now announced, in comprehensive detail, the standard liveries for locomotives, coaching and wagon rolling stock and for road vehicles which will be adopted as soon as is practicable.

RAIL VEHICLES

Express passenger steam and electric locomotives will be light blue with black and white lining applicable to the following classes –

LMR – Class 7P
ER & NER – A1, A3, A4, W1
WR – King
SR – Merchant Navy
ScR – Class 7P, A3, A4, A10

Selected express passenger steam locomotives will be dark green with black and orange lining applicable to the following classes –
LMR – Royal Scot, 5X converted 5XP Jubilee and Patriot
ER & NER – A2, B2, B3, B17
WR – Castle, Star

U No 31624 leaves Southampton Central with a Cheltenham train via Andover thence the MSWJ route. The headcode is a Southern Region 'route' code - one lamp under the chimney and one over the right hand buffer - indicating the service was from Southampton to Andover via Redbridge. North of Andover Junction the MSWJ proper commenced meaning the train was then on WR metals. Accordingly the headcode would change to the standard one lamp under the chimney for a stopping passenger train. The coaches are WR vehicles painted in 'blood and custard' the two leading vehicles at least being 'Toplights'. *S C Townroe*

Another A1 4-6-2, this time No 60149 *Armadis* with a down express. This engine was new in May 1949 and spent the first seven years of its life based at Grantham and Kings Cross. It moved to Doncaster in September 1958 remaining there until ceasing to work in June 1964. Two Mk1 vehicles in dual BR livery are visible. *Ken Wightman*

SR – West Country, Battle of Britain, Lord Nelson, King Arthur
ScR – Royal Scot, 5XP Jubilee, A2

Passenger and mixed traffic steam (tank and tender) and mixed traffic electric locomotives not included above will be black with red, cream and grey lining

Freight steam (tank and tender), electric shunting and diesel shunting locomotives will be unlined black
Diesel mainline locomotives will be black with aluminium lining and bogies

Mainline corridor coaches, compo brakes, third brakes, first brakes and also brake vans for use on principal passenger trains will be crimson lake with cream panels and with lining in gold and black

Coaches for local steam hauled trains and passenger train vans will be crimson lake with gold and black lining

Multiple Unit electric coaches will be unlined green

Wagons – unfitted will be dark battleship grey, fitted/piped will be orange brown, insulated will be stone (white where available). All wagons will have black underframes and undergear. Lettering and markings will be white Gill Sans Medium type except on insulated stock which will have black lettering.

Containers will be orange brown except insulated containers which will be stone until white paint becomes available

ROAD VEHICLES

Motor and horse drawn parcels vans except as below will have bodies and cabs in crimson below the waist line and cream above. Roofs will be cream, the chassis, wheels, mudguards and lamps (except plated) will be black. Interiors will be light stone.

Motor Horse Boxes will be crimson with cream roofs, the remainder being as above.

Cattle vehicles will be natural finish or paint with cream roofs, the remainder as above

Horse Drays will be black throughout

Trailers will be crimson

The lettering of road vehicles will be for flat vehicles and trailers 'British Railways' on the sides. Vans, half tilts and sided vehicles will have a totem on the sides. Horse boxes will have a totem and "Express Horse-Box Hire Service" on the sides. All vehicles will have the totem on the front of the cab and on the rear above the shutters or tail doors.

Precise measurements of the lettering for locomotive numbers and its positioning on cabsides is provided as per the diagram on page 4. The BR crest which all locomotives will carry should be placed centrally on the appropriate panels one left hand and one right hand so that the lion always faces forward although the position can be varied slightly to avoid bolt or rivet heads. Cab roofs and all handrails will be black, buffer beams and casings to be signal red. Frame extensions, smokeboxes, saddles, outside steam pipes and cylinder clothing to be black in all cases. Smoke deflectors should be black and unlined in all cases except the SR pacific classes.

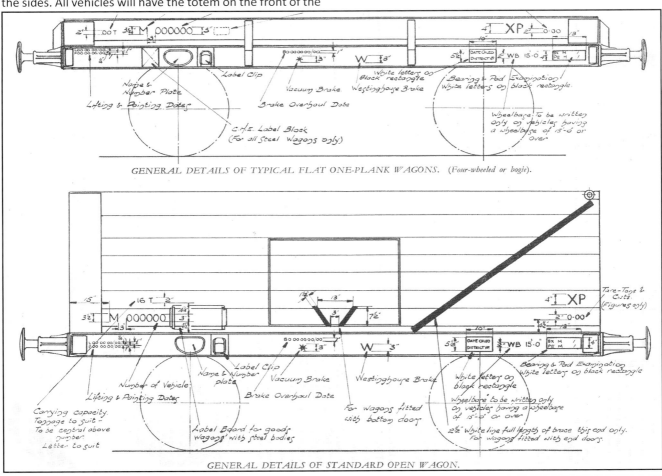

GENERAL DETAILS OF TYPICAL FLAT ONE-PLANK WAGONS. (Four-wheeled or bogie).

GENERAL DETAILS OF STANDARD OPEN WAGON.

British Railways Colour Schemes

From *The Railway Gazette* 1949.
Attributed to 'W.D.G.'

Pl*um and spilt milk*
Chocolate and cream
The Railway's become
A gourmet's dream

With engines green
As astringent lime
Or blue; they ran
To the sea on time

It could not last
On our homeward way
The engines were finished
In rust and in grey.

Beyer-Garratt on the Lickey

The U1 class Beyer-Garratt 2-8-8-2 locomotive of the former LNER No. 69999 has departed from its customary duties assisting trains up the 1 in 40 Worsborough incline near Barnsley and has been loaned to the Midland region for trials on the Lickey bank south of Birmingham.

This incline which is the steepest sustained adhesion worked gradient on BR stretches for two miles at 1 in 36.7 (2.65%) requiring the services of banking locomotives to assist the heaviest trains up the grade. With a tractive effort of 43,315 lb., *Big Bertha* as the 0-10-0 No. 58100 was known, had acted as resident banker from 1919 in tandem with 3F 0-6-0 tank locomotives. The trials of the Garratt, which had a tractive effort of a colossal 72,940 lb., lasted until 1950 during which time it initially worked chimney-first but after difficulty was experienced in buffering up to passenger trains it was turned to run cab-first up the bank with the additional aid of an electric headlight.

Despite changing the direction of travel, the crews still had great problems with visibility from the cab, particularly after dark, and the Garratt was returned to Derby Works yard where it stayed for some months until transferred to Mexborough in November 1950 where it was placed in storage.

During its sojourn on the Lickey, enginemen had experienced many problems with it including difficulty in getting the boiler to steam in spite of a variety of firing techniques being tried. There were no problems with its power output however although at times it was almost too much for the task in hand and on one occasion it managed to telescope the rear coach of the train it was assisting! (*Ed: In 1952 it was sent to Gorton Works preparatory to a return to the Lickey. However, it remained at Gorton for three years whilst attempts were made to convert it to oil burning. These came to nothing and in June 1955 it resumed work on the Lickey Incline this time with an improved electric headlight but by September it was stored at Bromsgrove returning to Gorton the following month. It was officially withdrawn on 23 December 1955 and transferred to Doncaster Works where it was scrapped early in 1956*).

Bromsgrove plays host to Class U1 No. 69999 pushing hard at the rear of a passenger service. From the angle of the coaches in the distance one can readily appreciate the severe gradient encountered here. *Neville Stead*

On 18 June 1955, No. 69999 was photographed at Gorton just prior to a brief return to the Lickey. *Peter Gray*

Back at its rightful home. The regular Lickey banker, No. 58100 is seen here at Blackwell. *Henry Cartwright*

Through the Porthole: BR's new all-steel coaches

The construction of integral all steel welded coaches for locomotive haulage had been initiated by the LMS as early as 1938 but a combination of WW2 and steel rationing had seen the programme interrupted and it was not until 1949 that the first examples began to appear from Derby Works.

In an echo of the famous 1930s streamlined stock that accompanied the visit of the 'Coronation Scot' to the USA the distinctive 'porthole' style windows for the lavatory compartments were incorporated into the new design which owed much to the influence of Stanier.

Built to lot No. 1499, the first all steel composite coach was numbered M24500M and very attractive it looked with a more rounded profile than was possible with earlier timber framed stock. With four 1st. class and three 3rd. Class compartments each seating six passengers, the total complement was 42 and there was a lavatory compartment with the porthole frosted glass window provided at each end of the coach.

There were four doors on the corridor side and two doors at the vestibule ends on the opposite side. This prototype coach was part of an initial order of 75 for mainline service.

Despite the popular belief that the first 75 coaches were finished in LMS livery but without the LMS lettering, none of them ever carried company livery when new but were finished in BR's new colours of carmine and cream. The steel side panels were supported upon a steel frame whilst this design would go on to influence the new BR Mark 1 type.

A further 75 were constructed to Lot 1500 followed by 90 more constructed to Lot 1586 along with a further 20 vestibule open first class coaches built at Wolverton to Lot 1503 this time containing a pair of lavatories at one end with therefore just one porthole window on each side.

All steel coaches had long been a feature of USA railroads and in late 1947 an American stainless steel coach built by the Budd Co. of Philadelphia for the Pressed Steel Co. of Cowley in Oxford was shipped to the UK. The coach framing contained structural members which, like the roof and side structures and the exterior panels, were made of stainless steel. The bogies and brakes however were of the standard British type and weighing in at 29 tons 5 cwt. the coach was 63ft. 6 ins. in length.

Of course all steel coaches were nothing new as the Southern Railway had introduced welded steel coaches (4SUB) in 1941 as part of their suburban electric multiple unit stock. The Motspur Park accident of November 1947 when two electric units collided in fog due to a fogman's error and where three passengers and one staff member who was travelling in one of the coaches on duty were killed, demonstrated the strength of the body of such vehicles. Although the bogies had been ripped off the all steel coach, which had been turned upside down by the impact, its structural integrity remained and this undoubtedly helped to save the lives of many of the passengers inside.

On the LMS all steel construction had also featured in the earlier Southport electric multiple unit stock dating from 1939. (*Ed: A couple of examples of the 60ft. coaches still exist. No. 24617 which served on the WR until 1968 can now be found on the Severn Valley Railway and No. 24725 is located on the Scottish Railway Preservation Society site at Bo'ness*).

Preserved Severn Valley Railway coach No. 24617 in LMS livery. *Wikipedia Creative Commons licence*

Final 'Aberdare' withdrawal

In the summer of 1949 the last quartet of 'Aberdares', Nos. 2620, 2651, 2655 and 2667, could be found still at work in the Birmingham area with a couple allocated to Stourbridge Junction shed. However, with the withdrawal of No. 2667 from Pontypool Road shed in October the last of these 2-6-0s was withdrawn from service by the WR.

Designed by William Dean, although with obvious Churchward influences, 80 examples of the 2600 and 2620 classes, numbered 2601-80, were constructed during the period 1901-1906 following the prototype No. 33 built in 1900 which was renumbered 2600 in 1912.

They were a freight version of the 3300 and 4120 4-4-0 'Bulldog' and 'Atbara' classes and were used mainly for hauling coal trains from the South Wales valleys, particularly around Aberdare in the Cynon valley hence their nickname, to Swindon.

The class were initially paired with 3,000 gallon tenders although a few did have tenders of 3,500 gallons and from the late 1930s onwards 4,000 gallon tenders from

withdrawn ROD 2-8-0s were made available to the surviving class members.

Withdrawn from 1934 onwards five examples were formally withdrawn in 1939 but stored as a strategic reserve during WW2 being reinstated to traffic the following year. In the mid 1930s their primary coal hauling duties were taken over by the large 72xx class 2-8-2 tanks and by the mid 1940s they looked distinctly old fashioned with their full length outside mainframes and connecting rods reminiscent of their 4-4-0 'Bulldog' and 'Duke' class predecessors.

Top: Aberdare class No. 2651 rumbles through Oxford station northbound with a lengthy freight on an unrecorded date in 1948. It would be withdrawn from Gloucester Horton Road shed the following June being one of the final examples then in traffic. The engine is attached to a former R.O.D. tender. *Alec Ford*

Bottom: On 27 February 1939 No. 2620 was photographed inside the old shed at Stourbridge Junction from where it would be withdrawn ten years later in August 1949. This view well illustrates the dated appearance of this outside frame turn of the century Dean design. *Peter Pescod*

Last of the Patriot rebuilds

A number of the Patriot 4-6-0s, the initial pair of which was introduced in 1930 as a Fowler rebuild of two L&NWR Claughtons and with a further 50 constructed as new locomotives again to a Fowler design in 1933, have been the subject of an LMS rebuilding programme begun in 1946 under the stewardship of Ivatt which finished in 1949 under BR after 18 locomotives had been dealt with.

This new sub class would be known as Rebuilt Patriots and comprised the following locomotives –

No.	Name	Rebuilt
5530	Sir Frank Ree	10/46
5521	Rhyl	11/46
5526	Morecambe & Heysham	2/47
5514	Holyhead	3/47
5529	Stephenson	7/47
5540	Sir Robert Turnbull	10/47
5531	Sir Frederick Harrison	12/47
45532	Illustrious	6/48
45512	Bunsen	7/48
45525	Colwyn Bay	8/48
45527	Southport	9/48
45528		9/48
45535	Sir Herbert Walker K.C.B.	9/48
45523	Bangor	10/48
45536	Private W. Wood V.C.	11/48
45545	Planet	11/48
45534	E. Tootal Broadhurst	12/48
45522	Prestatyn	1/49

The power classification of the unrebuilt Patriots was uprated from 5XP to 6P5F and the rebuilt versions, which had a larger taper boiler, new cylinders and double chimney, was increased to 7P in 1951.

Rebuilt Patriot Class No. 45522 *Prestatyn* is seen in the Nuneaton area during the 1950s. *Alec Ford*

Rebuilt Patriot 4-6-0 No.45545 *Planet* with an 5A (Crewe North) shedplate was photographed in June 1958 outside Barrow-in-Furness shed. *Mikepost*

No. 20002 has charge of the up Newhaven Boat service seen here near Cooksbridge on the cut off line between Keymer Junction on the Brighton mainline and Lewes. *R C Riley*

Taking the route through Lewes to Keymer Junction on the Brighton to London mainline, No. 20002 heads an up boat train service on 7 August 1950. *R C Riley*

All change on the Newhaven boat trains

From the start of the summer timetable on 23 May 1949, boat trains connecting Victoria with Newhaven from where boats ply the English Channel to Dieppe will have new motive power.

For long the province of the famous Brighton Atlantics, latterly on their final mainline workings, and more recently the Schools class, these services will now be hauled by one of the trio of Co Co electrics or 'Hornbys' as they came to be known. The coaching sets attached to this service have been painted in the new BR standard livery of crimson lake and cream whilst two of the new locomotives are finished in green and one in blue. On 15 May, a few days prior to the start of the new timetable, the first run of an electrically hauled boat train service was entrusted to the charge of the most recently completed of the trio No. 20003.

Compared to the prior steam hauled service, journey time was noticeably reduced although an upper speed limit of 75 mph was then in force for electric locomotives. Indeed the first down journey arrived some 15 minutes early whilst the up train also succeeded in shaving 16½ minutes off the schedule.

The line to Newhaven and Seaford had been electrified by the Southern Railway back in 1935 and shortly after electric traction had been proposed, but not implemented, for the boat train services. It was not until July 1947 that the short section from Newhaven Town to the harbour station was electrified thus making possible the use of electric traction for the complete journey.

Under the watchful eye of a railway employee No. 20001 enters Cooksbridge station, the first station north of Lewes on the line to Keymer Junction, with the up 'Newhaven Boat' on 14 August 1955. *R C Riley*

Bulleid pacific No. 34006 *Bude* which successfully took part in the trials is seen at Sheffield Victoria in 1948 gaining some glances from local railwaymen no doubt unused to seeing such a strange looking beast. *Neville Stead*

1948 Interchange Trials Results

THE RESULTS ARE IN!

Following the locomotive interchange trials of last year BR have now reported on the findings although it is not intended to publish the results for general consumption due to the cost of production and the fact that much of the report consists of tables of data, descriptions of the test and loading arrangements, and consumption of coal and water statistics for the various locomotives involved.

The stated objective of these comparative trials was to identify the best features amongst the Big Four in terms of locomotive design so that they could be incorporated into the planned range of twelve BR Standard designs. It was not the intention of BR to continue to produce four varieties of different types of locomotive to suit every BR region but rather to come up with a standardised design suitable for all regions. However, doubts have been expressed about the scientific rigour involved in the trials and although they were undoubtedly a useful publicity exercise and an opportunity for BR to show the unity of the new nationalised organisation, many observers felt that

due to political reasons - for example H G Ivatt was the only CME to remain in post after 1949 - former LMS practice was likely to become dominant in decisions about the shape of locomotive building in the future.

It was recognised that although dynamometer cars were used on the tests to record data, further testing on the stationary plants at Swindon and on the new facility at Rugby would be required.

On the WR due to the nature of the grate and smokebox arrangements on former GWR locomotives tailored as they were to Welsh steam coal, further tests using this coal source would be required to give a fair comparison of performance. Amongst the express passenger locomotives coal consumption ratios i.e. coal total weight in lb. / work done in hp/hr ranged from 3.06 for the A4 to 3.60 for the Merchant Navy and in the mixed traffic class from 3.54 for the Black 5 to 4.11 for the West Country class. On the freight side the lowest figure was 3.37 for the O1 2-8-0 with the highest being the Austerity 2-8-0 at 3.77. Similarly the water consumption ratio i.e. water in total weight lb / work done

Royal Scot Class No. 46162 *Queen's Westminster Rifleman* hauling the 7.50am service from Leeds approaches Finsbury Park at 12:10pm during the exchange trials on 20 April 1948. *Alec Swain*

in hp/hr again showed the A4 to be the lowest at 24.32 with the highest again being the Merchant Navy at 30.43. For the mixed traffic classes the B1 was the lowest at 27.64 and the West Country the highest at 32.64. The lowest freight locomotive was again the O1 with the highest once more being the Austerity 2-8-0.

Given the restricted nature of the information made available to the general public, reliance had to be placed upon professional railway commentators to give an opinion on how the various locomotives had fared in the trials. It was generally agreed that the Royal Scot class had performed particularly well standing up strongly against the more powerful pacifics. The King class had suffered from not using Welsh coal in the trials but subsequently they achieved a 6.5% reduction in average coal consumption and an even better reduction of 17.7% was noted with the Hall class when Welsh coal was used in subsequent trials.

West Country No. 34006 *Bude* put in excellent performances between Marylebone and Manchester as did Merchant Navy No. 35017 *Belgian Marine* between Penrith and Preston on the West Coast Main Line gaining several minutes on the schedule allowed. A4s also did well in terms of low coal consumption over the South Devon banks. So in summary something good could be said about representatives of all four pre nationalisation companies!

The Railway Executive concluded from these trials that no limit should be placed on its standard designs to cater for any particular characteristics of the routes over which they will operate. This view was borne out by the way in which locomotives from the four companies operated satisfactorily over 'foreign' metals being able to haul their booked loads to the laid down schedules without problem.

Many features of the four companies' designs have been identified for possible incorporation into the new standard classes, such as the use of the largest boilers possible, within weight limit restrictions, so as to provide ample reserve power to cater for all eventualities. Wide fireboxes in the larger locomotives giving the highest combustion efficiency were also considered desirable as were various ashpan and firebox arrangements catering for a wide variety in coal quality.

Finally good riding and low track wear were also deemed important and the adoption of various design features such as roller bearings for example to achieve these aims would also be considered. These tests of course only provided data on performance 'out on the road' and will need to be read in conjunction with data on the cost of locomotive construction, maintenance and repair costs and upon availability for traffic in service.

No. 46162 seen again but this time handling the 8.30am service from Plymouth on 28 May 1948. It is photographed here going well near Ealing at 1.43pm. *Alec Swain*

'Capitals Limited' Non-stop to Scotland

Although the 'Flying Scotsman' with its traditional 10am departure from King's Cross was reinstated after WW2 it was later slowed from a non-stop service to one that had three intermediate stops. In the summer of 1949 BR acknowledging that a non-stop service would prove popular introduced the 'Capitals Limited' departing London at 9:30am with an arrival into Edinburgh eight hours later, the down service leaving Waverley at 9:45am. By 1951 the journey time was down to 7 hours 20 minutes whilst in 1953 the service was renamed the 'Elizabethan' which saw a further reduction to just 6 hours and 45 minutes, ultimately reducing to 6½. hours in 1954.

Top: No. 60024 *Kingfisher* hurries the down 'Capitals Limited' northwards through Huntingdon on 29 July 1952. *Eric Sawford*

Right: Another A4 pacific, this one No. 60034, renamed *Lord Faringdon* from *Peregrine* the previous year, heads the up 'Capitals Limited' express at Riccall, between York and Selby in July 1949. *George Ellis*

No. 60009 *Union of South Africa* was photographed with the 'Capitals Limited' near Huntingdon, which was then known as Huntingdon North. *Eric Sawford*

EYEMOUTH RE-OPENING

Following the disastrous East Coast Main line floods of August 1948, featured in the previous issue of *Railway Times*, the branch from Burnmouth to Eyemouth re-opened on 29 June 1949.

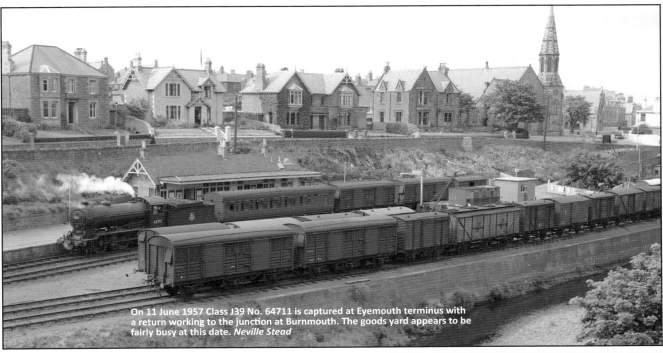

On 11 June 1957 Class J39 No. 64711 is captured at Eyemouth terminus with a return working to the junction at Burnmouth. The goods yard appears to be fairly busy at this date. *Neville Stead*

Class J21 No. 65078 is at the head of a service from Eyemouth for Burnmouth. This image is undated but this 0-6-0 acquired its BR number in October 1948 and was withdrawn in March 1957. *George Bett*

At the junction at Burnmouth Class J39 No. 64844 waits with the branch train for Eyemouth on 13 August 1960 whilst a Berwick bound train occupies the up platform. *Neville Stead*

MELTHAM-LOCKWOOD CLOSURE

This former L&YR branchline from Meltham to Lockwood, situated on the Penistone to Huddersfield line, was closed to passengers on 23 May 1949.

An undated view of the terminus at Meltham. *Henry Priestley*

HADDINGTON-LONGNIDDRY CLOSURE

This former North British Railway branch line was closed on 5 December 1949.

This view of Haddington station and goods shed dates from 1949. Note the SR cattle wagon on the left seemingly far from home at this Scottish outpost. Under Maunsell the SR constructed 299 of these vans between 1930-39, with a further batch built under Bulleid from 1947. Although short distance cattle traffic was largely lost to road during the inter-war years longer distance movements declined more slowly and were quite common until the early 1960s. *Neville Stead*

BODDAM – ELLON CLOSURE

This former GNoS branch which ran from Ellon on the line from Aberdeen to Peterhead and Fraserburgh to the coastal resort of Boddam and which had closed to passengers on 31 October 1932 finally shut its doors to freight from 1 January 1949. One of the main objectives behind construction of the line had been to serve the famous Cruden Bay hotel but the season was short on the bracing Aberdeenshire coast and traffic never lived up to expectations with the hotel being requisitioned by the military in 1940. It would never re-open and was sold for demolition in 1947.

Three giants of steam retire

BR LOSES A TRIO OF CMEs

This year saw the loss of three eminent Chief Mechanical Engineers (CMEs) – Frederick Hawksworth (WR), Arthur Peppercorn (ER) and Oliver Bulleid (SR) all of whom retired from BR in 1949. From the Big Four this just left George Ivatt (LMR) in post in addition to Robert Riddles who, with two assistants, effectively took over the role of CME for BR in 1948 overseeing the production of the new Standard classes. Ivatt retired in 1951.

Frederick William Hawksworth. 1884-1976

Joining the GWR as an apprentice in 1898 he was to spend his entire working life at Swindon. He became an apprentice draughtsman in 1905 under Churchward becoming one of the small coterie known as 'Churchward's Bright Young Men'. He became involved in such revolutionary designs as *The Great Bear*. Following Churchward's retirement in 1921 he became Chief Draughtsman to Churchward's successor Collett under whom he worked on perhaps the ultimate in GWR design - the King class. Following the departure of William Stanier to the LMS in 1932 he was appointed Assistant to the CME soon afterwards becoming Principal Assistant. Collett's reluctance to give up the CME's post resulted in Hawksworth's lateness in taking up this position. Collett hung on until he was 70 before retiring so Hawksworth had to wait until 1941 before becoming CME one of only six holders of this post over the last 100 years.

Whilst continuing in the design tradition with which he had been involved throughout his career he also made some important changes including extending superheat to a number of locomotive classes and in techniques of welded construction as found expression in his slab sided tender design. Many years before BR had its own testing plant at Rugby Hawksworth was instrumental in modernising the stationary locomotive testing plant at Swindon. His first design, the Modified Hall, was a significant development of the Collett design with increased superheat and a radically different cylinder and frame construction. Post-war there came several new designs including the County Class and his taper boilered 94xx Class pannier tank which was built in considerable numbers largely by outside contractors.

Perhaps his most radical design was the 15xx class which is the subject of the article on page 27. The last Hawksworth design was a rather conventional pannier tank the 1600 class. He was also involved in ordering non steam motive power represented by the GWR diesel shunters and two experimental gas turbine locomotives. He continued to work on designs right up until retiring at the end of 1949 after which he became chairman of Swindon magistrates from 1951 until 1959 and he was made a freeman of the borough in 1960. He died in Swindon in July 1976. With his retirement the post of CME disappeared and separate departments were created to spread the load covering mechanical and engineering, carriage and wagon, and motive power.

Arthur Henry Peppercorn. 1889-1951.

(Image courtesy the A1 Steam Locomotive Trust who were the builders of *Tornado* and who are currently constructing a P2).

Starting his career as an apprentice with the GNR at Doncaster, Arthur Peppercorn like Frederick Hawksworth was lucky enough to have caught the attention of the CME, in this case Nigel Gresley, with whom he would go on to form a close almost familial relationship until the untimely death of Gresley in 1941.

Although Peppercorn was considered as a potential successor it fell to Edward Thompson, already 60 years of age, to be offered the post. Peppercorn eventually got his chance in July 1946 when he took over from Thompson as CME. Although a modest man he could appreciate the limitations of the Gresley conjugated valve gear and the major flaws of the Thompson style designed locomotives. Completing several projects begun by Thompson and cancelling some others Peppercorn, or 'Pepp' as he was affectionately known by his staff, revised the original design and constructed 70 of the class K1, he continued the construction of the B1 and stopped any further rebuilding of the A10 class into the A1/1 specification. As illustrated in the article on page 19 of Issue 1, his most significant contributions to locomotive development on the ER were his A1 and A2 classes. These two designs addressed the limitations of both the Thompson and Gresley pacifics, producing locomotives which were the masters of almost every task asked of them without the drawbacks of centre big-end bearing overheat, leaking steam pipe connections, frame fractures or any of the other difficulties that were associated with previous LNER Pacifics.

The real strength of the Peppercorn pacifics lay in their reliability, durability and efficiency in operation. He occupied the post of CME for three and a half years and his retirement was marked, not by the quiet send off this modest man would have wanted, but by a dinner party at which toasts were raised and a model of No. 525 which carried his name presented to him.

Unfortunately his retirement proved to be short lived as he died in March 1951.

Oliver Vaughan Snell Bulleid. 1882-1970.

Completing his apprenticeship with the Great Northern Railway under H. A. Ivatt at Doncaster, he became initially the assistant to the Locomotive Running Superintendent and a year later the Doncaster Works manager. In 1908 he left to work abroad as a Test Engineer with Westinghouse later marrying Ivatt's youngest daughter. Working for the Board of Trade arranging exhibitions in Brussels, Paris and Turin he was able to travel widely in Europe and in 1912 he rejoined the GNR as Personal Assistant to Gresley. Following an interruption for war service he returned to the GNR as the Manager of the Wagon and Carriage Works. With Gresley appointed CME of the new LNER at the grouping Bulleid resumed his previous role as assistant and had a hand in many of Gresley's designs.

In 1937, after the retirement of Richard Maunsell, Bulleid accepted the post of Chief Mechanical Engineer of the Southern Railway reportedly at an annual salary of £3,000 (£142,000 in today's money). Oversight of the construction of three 350 hp 0-6-0 diesel electric shunters previously ordered by Maunsell proved to be his first task upon taking office. He was also responsible for a number of front end improvements to the layout of some of the existing steam express passenger locomotives on the railway such as the 'Lord Nelson' class which improved performance considerably. The following year he got the go ahead to construct his most striking achievement the 'Merchant Navy' class which although inspired by his previous mentor Gresley incorporated some of the most modern aspects, such as a partially welded boiler and firebox and thermic siphons allied to a high working pressure.

One of the less successful aspects was the chain driven valve gear immersed in an oil bath which, given the poor maintenance experienced during the war years, gave trouble plus the fact that there turned out to be design errors in the casing used for the oil bath leading to leaks and the occasional fire. Smaller and lighter pacifics of the 'West Country' and 'Battle of Britain' classes followed. His other major steam locomotive design the Q1 'Austerity' freight locomotive presented just as radical an appearance as the air smoothed pacifics.

Apart from his involvement in the production of the two diesel electric locomotives Nos. 10201 and 10202 he also played a major role in the electrification of the SR, designing multiple units and electric locomotives. His coach designs were attractive and comfortable to ride in, aspects of which were later incorporated into the BR Mark 1 design, although his double deck EMU, see article on page 42, and his Tavern

Car, see article on page 33, were less appreciated. His final steam locomotive design was the unconventional 'Leader' the design of which took on the appearance of a diesel locomotive. The most charitable description of the concept is perhaps 'innovative but unsuccessful' and after Bulleid departed BR the project was quietly dropped.

Leaving BR he was appointed CME of C.I.É., the nationalised transport authority of the Irish Republic having been their consulting engineer since 1949. He pioneered CIE's first major dieselisation programme thus beginning a transformation of motive power in Eire although the locomotives proved rather unreliable and most were later re-engined. Continuing his maverick streak and, due to Ireland's chronic shortage of coal reserves, he developed two prototype peat burning steam locomotives one along the lines of the Leader design. He was appointed CBE in the 1949 New Year Honours List and retired in 1958. In the late 1960s he moved to Malta where he died in 1970. Always controversial he was, as the Times described him, '...the last truly original and progressive mechanical engineer of the steam locomotive era in Britain'.

Pannier Tanks old and new

The pannier tank had a long history on the GWR beginning with the conversion of saddle tanks in the early 1900s when Belpaire fireboxes, which could not easily accommodate saddle tanks, were fitted to locomotives of classes such as the 850 and 1901.

Many hundreds of traditional pannier tanks were produced over the years with the final members of the 9400 Class not appearing until 1956. In 1949 however, a new look was achieved with the Hawksworth designed 1500 Class which departed from GWR tradition in a visually significant way. They were provided with outside cylinders allied to Walschaerts valve gear which made virtually the whole of the running gear accessible from ground level thus making maintenance much easier and removing the need for an engine pit which was normally available only at depots.

This was particularly useful as the primary purpose of the design was to enable long periods of shunting to be undertaken at marshalling yards without returning to shed. The remainder of the design closely followed GWR practice utilising a standard No. 10 boiler, with pressure set at 200lbs/sq. In., this being of a similar type to that fitted to the 94xx pannier tanks and to the 22xx class 0-6-0s. However, the absence of footplating at the front end together with the front bufferbeam standing out on brackets in isolation gives the design an almost 'austerity' feel which is amplified by the exposure of the front ends of the cylinders and of the valve chests and cast saddle supporting the smokebox.

Whilst the provision of outside cylinders and a Walschaerts gear to 0-6-0 tank locomotives was certainly unusual it was not the first time that this had been applied on GWR locomotives. The 1361 Class of saddle tanks and the 1366 Class of pannier tanks both exhibited outside cylinders and as far back as 1926 the 1101 Class 0-4-0 dock tank was endowed with a Walschaerts gear.

They were naturally enough constructed at Swindon and, numbered 1500-9, entered service between June and September 1949. Weighing in at a hefty 58 tons 4 cwt the design was route restricted, colour code red, and in service were liable to become unstable at speed due to their short wheelbase. However they were not designed for speed and this short wheelbase of just 12ft. 10ins., compared to the 15ft. 6ins. of the regular pannier tanks, did allow them to negotiate curves as sharp as 3 chains radius at slow speed. They carried 3½ tons of coal and 1,350 gallons of water and were rated as power classification 'C', or 4F in BR terms. Aside from their work in marshalling yards they were later to become synonymous with empty coaching stock movements at Paddington.

No. 1502 shunting a freight is seen at Didcot. Note the shunter's wagon hitched behind the locomotive. *James Harold*

Light engine No. 1503 enters Paddington on 7 May 1955 where they were a common sight hauling empty coaching stock. *Eric Sawford*

No. 1503 is seen by the coaling stage at Old Oak Common shed. *Derek Potten*

No. 8487 takes water at Old Oak Common shed in 1963.
Roger Palmer

Old Oak Common roundhouse accommodates 940xx Class 0-6-0PT No. 9455 alongside 57xx Class pannier No. 9707.
Barry Richardson

Of more traditional design, although featuring taper boilers, were the new Class 9400 pannier tanks 200 of which were constructed by outside contractors.

Messrs. W G Bagnall Ltd. built 80 of these and the first, No. 8400, entered service at the end of August. The Yorkshire Engine Co and Robert Stephenson & Hawthorn constructed the remainder of the order. Although using WR working drawings they differ slightly from the first ten of the 94xx class, which were superheated and built at Swindon in 1947, as they do not feature superheaters.

The new locomotives were fitted with a standard GWR No. 10 boiler set to a working pressure of 200lbs/sq.in. weighing in at 55 tons 7cwt. Delivery from the contractors was slow with the final batch not being delivered until 1956 thus representing the final pre-nationalisation design to be constructed.

The first withdrawals took place just three years later in 1959 as much of the work for which they were designed was rapidly disappearing. Several examples went on to work on banking duties on the Lickey incline where at times four engines were needed to push the heaviest trains.

BR Rolling Stock construction programme 1949

In 1948 BR had inherited a huge variety of rolling stock from the four mainline companies including 20,023 steam locomotives of no less than 448 different designs many of them dating back more than 70 years to Victorian times. In addition there were 16 electric, 53 diesel, 2 petrol, 47 service and 7 narrow gauge locomotives.

Total passenger coaching stock at the start of 1948 was just over 40,000 vehicles with non-passenger stock amounting to just over 56,000 units.

The greatest number was understandably freight stock, no less than a substantial 1.2 million goods wagons half of which came from privately owned fleets.

In 1949 there was still much work to do to replace rolling stock damaged or worn out in war time and to cater for the increase in traffic following the lifting of wartime restrictions In consequence BR announced the following construction programme for the year which in summary consisted of 465 locomotives, 1,972 coaches and 27,225 wagons.

Locomotives						
Builder	LMR	SR	WR	E&NER	Contractors	Totals
Class 5 4-6-0	32					32
'Castle' 4-6-0			10			10
'Hall' 4-6-0			10			10
'B1' 4-6-0				18	10	28
'A1' 4-6-2				28		28
'Merchant Navy' 4-6-2		2				2
'WC / BB' 4-6-2		15				15
2-6-2T	30		10			40
2-6-4T	30				24	54
Class 4 2-6-0	27					27
'K1' 2-6-0					70	70
0-6-0T			45	15	50	110
'Leader' class 0-6-6-0		5				5
350hp diesel	13					13
800hp diesel					1	1
Diesel mechanical shunter		1				1
Diesel electric shunter			1			1
350hp diesel electric		15				15
Mainline diesel electric		2				2
Gas Turbine					1	1
Total	132	40	76	61	156	465

Coaches						
Steam Stock						
Builder	**LMR**	**SR**	**WR**	**E&NER**	**Contractors**	**Totals**
1st 3rd & Composite	443	222	109	180	291	1245
Restaurant, Buffer & Kitchen cars		8		14		22
Sleeping cars			4	1		5
PO sorting vans	7			6		13
Luggage & Fish vans, Carriage trucks etc	90	21	10	66		187
Electric stock						
Motor coaches		100				100
Trailer coaches		100				100
3-car sets					300	300
Total	**540**	**451**	**123**	**267**	**591**	**1972**

Wagons						
Builder	**LMR**	**SR**	**WR**	**E&NE**	**Contractors**	**Totals**
Open	327	1627	50	2350		4354
Covered	2920	750	496			4166
Bolster	350		50	700		1100
Plate	74			250		324
Cattle	150	150	400	1100	100	1900
Mineral *	1333			1700	10215	13248
Special **	68		52	27	17	164
Fish				400		400
Brake vans	325		112	290		727
Service vehicles	160	49	558	1		842
Total	**5707**	**2576**	**1718**	**6818**	**10406**	**27225**

66% of the locomotives, 70% of the coaches and 62% of the wagons will be constructed by BR in house.

Of the 500 electric coaches to be constructed 276 will be for the new Shenfield electrification scheme, 24 for Manchester – Sheffield suburban services and 200 for the SR's suburban services.

* Of the mineral wagon total 4601 will be of the hopper type with bottom doors to enable speedy discharge.

** Special wagons will be constructed to meet the specific needs of particular industries to cater for such items as long timber and steel.

This view of one of the dining saloons (S7840) of a tavern car set named *The Dolphin* taken at Clapham Junction in 1949 illustrates the small high level windows that caused so much controversy. It is seen here in crimson and cream livery. Note also the two vehicles were semi-permanently coupled by means of a buck-eye with no buffers between the two cars. *Transport Library*

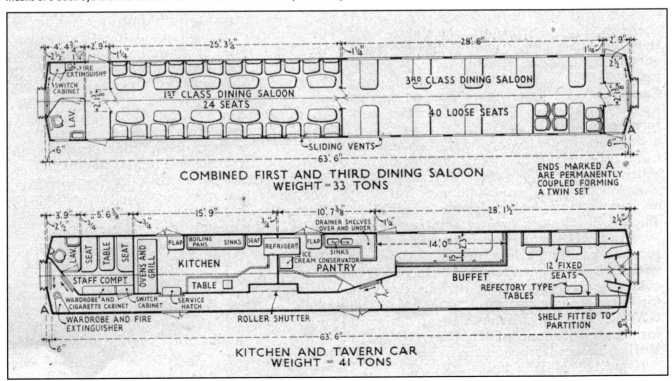

Tavern Cars

_There is a tavern in the town, in the town
And there my dear love sits him down, sits him down
And drinks his wine 'mid laughter free
And never, never thinks of me_

(Traditional folk song)

Passengers boarding the 10:35 am 'Atlantic Coast Express' from Waterloo from 28 May 1949 were in for something of a shock when they later made their way along to the dining car section of the train. For instead of the usual Restaurant Car they found a 'Kitchen and Tavern Car' allied to a 'Combined First and Third Class Dining Saloon'.

These restaurant-buffet two car sets were the result of a joint venture between the Hotels Executive and the Railway Executive of the British Transport Commission (BTC) with design being entrusted to that Southern Region maverick – Oliver Bulleid who, it is believed, based the design on 'The Chequers' inn in Pulborough in Sussex.

The eight twin units were constructed at Lancing Carriage Works with two being destined for the Southern Region and six for the Eastern Region. Adapted from the traditional folk song quoted above, publicity for these new coaches used the tag line 'There is a tavern on the train'.

The external appearance was to say the least somewhat bizarre with faux brickwork lined out on the new crimson lake livery on the lower panels whilst on the upper panels mock 'Tudorbethan' half timbered vertical black panels broke up the underlying cream panelling. A vitreous enamel plate was attached to the exterior proclaiming itself to be one of the following inn signs – 'White Horse', 'Jolly Tar', 'Dolphin', 'Three Plovers', 'The Bull', 'The Salutation', 'The Green Man' and 'The Crown'. Strangely there was no 'King's Head', 'Red Lion' or 'Royal Oak' the three most popular UK pub names. The signs were painted by David Cobb, a marine artist, and John Main. (Folklore has it that Bulleid had instructed the Eastleigh works manager to go on a literal pub-crawl around Hampshire to find suitable names.)

The interior design of the Tavern Car was just as odd with dark oak, particularly uncomfortable, fixed settles seating twelve placed against the walls with tables in front. The tiny windows with imitation leaded panes were set high up on the coach sides thus denying seated customers anything of a view of the passing scene and were perhaps included to speed up the throughput of customers who would not wish to linger in these rather unfamiliar somewhat claustrophobic surroundings. 'Antique' square metal lanterns were suspended from dark oak roof beams set into a rough plastered effect white ceiling. Floor covering mimicked the black and red tiling found in many a country pub whilst at one end of the car was a cocktail bar and snack counter finished in stainless steel and a rather charming plastic!

Temperature was controlled by the thermostatic system of pressure ventilation. To add the finishing touch suspended from one of the roof beams was a small reproduction inn sign echoing the monstrosity seen outside.

Public reaction was to say the least rather negative with that well known cartoonist and architectural historian Osbert Lancaster of the _Daily Express_ calling the concept "the height of absurdity".

Indeed during a Parliamentary debate in June, Tom Driberg MP said "Words fail me to express the full horror which I felt when the announcement was made by B.R. of the cars which they described as being 'mock Tudor style'".

Another politician, the gloriously named Skeffington Lodge MP dismissed the concept as "bogus sentimentality". However, the Parliamentary Secretary to the Ministry of Transport, one Jim Callaghan, defended the concept stating that "the use to which these Tavern Cars have been put has exceeded the wildest expectations in revenue that the Railway Executive ever hoped to get." He went on to say "nobody likes them except the public and the public have flocked to them. There has been a lot of heat and exaggerated language used by people who have not been within half a mile of them."

Passing through swing doors, with leaded lights of course, one reached the kitchen and pantry section and then into the second coach the dining section of which had seats, apparently upholstered in pink and silver brocade, for 24 first class and 40 third class passengers. Lighting here was concealed fluorescent and the half timbered effect has been improved slightly with the use of light figured oak allied to buff coloured plastic wall panels. Seating again was radically different to the norm with seats facing inwards extending along the whole length of each side of the coach with separate tables for each pair of seats. Seating in third class is perhaps preferable being of the usual type with each diner having the luxury of an individual moveable chair. Coach bodies were of timber construction with steel panels and as much of the equipment as practicable was housed in the underframes below floor level to maximise circulation space for passengers.

The two coach units were not cheap to build with the eight sets costing £64,000, representing 23% of BR's restaurant

33

car budget of £281,000 for the year.

Mr Callaghan was also accurate in his words for they did indeed return the best takings of any catering vehicle on BR.

Opposition was not just voiced by the travelling public but also by the National United Temperance League and the Methodist church who were against the concept of alcohol on trains .

On the Eastern Region the sets were destined for the 'Master Cutler', 'South Yorkshireman', 'White Rose', 'Norfolkman' and the 'North Country Continental', the latter between Harwich and Liverpool.

Following a campaign threatening to boycott those cars based on the Eastern Region all the two car sets were concentrated on the Southern Region during the autumn of 1949 and in the following year were all rebuilt with conventional seating and windows. In 1959 a further £22,900 was spent on remodelling into conventional buffet style. There is a short silent clip available to view on the Pathe News website featuring the 'Jolly Tar' unit at Waterloo.

Above and opposite bottom - Third class dining.

Opposite top - First class dining.

No.	Name	Restaurant car No.
7895	The Bull	7833
7896	The Three Plovers	7834
7897	The Salutation	7835
7898	The Green Man	7836
7899	The Crown	7837
7892	The White Horse	7838
7893	The Jolly Tar	7839
7894	The Dolphin	7840

Left and right - Inn signs; the faux brickwork will be noted.

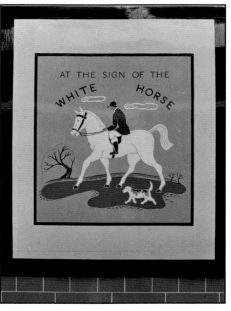

The buffet and bar area in the Kitchen Car of *The White Horse*. As with several of the interior views, these were no doubt posed for publicity purposes.

BR Standard cab layout

In the expectation that the first of the twelve new BR Standard locomotive types will enter service in 1951, towards the end of 1949 a completely new standardised layout was designed for the cabs of such locomotives. It combines 'best practice' from the regions together with the introduction of new ideas. Designed ergonomically around the requirements of operating crews a mock-up has been constructed at Crewe Works to test crew reaction and usability. With a cabside number of 70000, the full size mock up supported on trestles comprises the footplate and cab together with a section of boiler and tender. The replica was subsequently put on display at Marylebone in 1950 where it could be viewed by railwaymen and public alike.

The new design of the roomy cab affords maximum protection from the weather for the footplate crew and improves the working environment by keeping the cab as cool as possible through having the majority of the steam pipes and valves placed outside the cab. A sliding door is provided in the cab roof to aid ventilation and the side windows can also be opened. Visibility both forwards and backwards is improved by having the large front windows, which are moveable to aid cleaning, set at an angle to reduce glare. Rear visibility is helped by having windows set in the tender front. Vibration is also minimised by having the footplate floor extend right back to the tender and by securing the cab to the boiler rather than the frames thus reducing the relative movement encountered with the old design of moveable flap between locomotive and tender. All controls required by the driver are easily to hand such that he can operate them without leaving his seat. Similarly the fittings under the control of the fireman are also conveniently placed on his side of the cab. Locker accommodation has been improved and even includes a stainless steel cupboard for the crew's food items that have double doors to exclude dirt and grime.

Ease of accessibility has also been an important innovation by having the steam pipes and valves outside the cab as an aid to periodic maintenance and by having the rocking grate controls sunk below floor level covered by plates which fit flush to the cab floor thus reducing draughts and dust. The control for the self emptying ashpan doors is placed at ground level and the injectors are secured to the firebox in accessible positions.

(Ed: A similar cab mock up was later built by BR for No. 71000 and this is currently on display in the Science Museum collection).

Playing at Trains - BR's model railway

It might come as something of a surprise to learn that BR felt it worthwhile to have its own model railway which could be transported around the country to various exhibitions with the aim of increasing the interest of the public generally in BR and attracting schoolboys who might aspire to become future employees. The brochure, produced by the Railway Executive in 1949, explained that the layout had been assembled by specialist staff attached to the Executive with some components bought in from commercial firms. It was first exhibited at the Schoolboys' Own exhibition held at London's Royal Agricultural Hall from 1-19 January 1949.

Measuring some 30 x 15 feet and supported on tables with adjustable legs to suit any exhibition space, the three-rail track system was used with a wide variety of rolling stock being featured. Illuminated colour light signals were used rather than semaphores but with the caveat that, "it has been found impracticable to keep signal lights burning constantly as the life of the bulbs is too short!" The locomotives took power at 20v DC being supplied from AC mains through rectifiers. Electric points were worked by double solenoid point motors working on 20v AC.

The normal layout configuration is shown below.

Taking the opportunity to showcase some of the latest BR designs the model motive power operated on the layout included the following –

'Merchant Navy'
Sir William Stanier 'Coronation' pacific No. 46256
Diesel No. 10000
A H Peppercorn Class 'A2' pacific No. 60525
Class L1 2-6-4T
GWR County Class 4-6-0

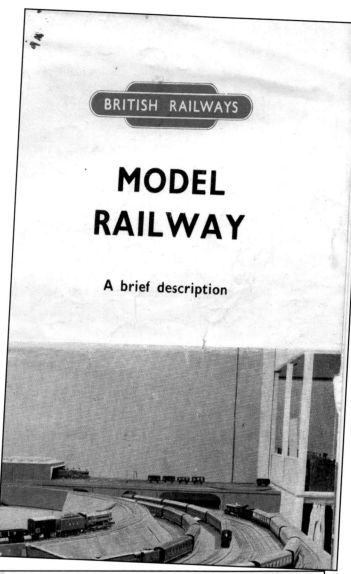

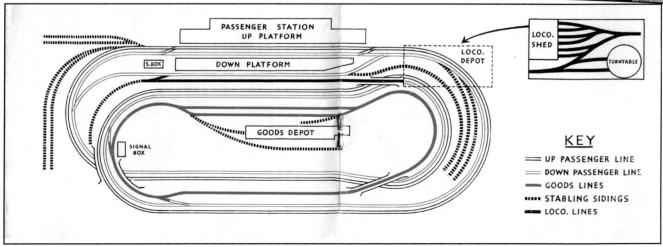

Coaching stock in the newly chosen liveries was also in evidence with six-coach mainline sets being provided in crimson lake and cream, chocolate and cream, green, teak and in red. Pullman cars with an Observation saloon and SR electric stock in green could also be seen. The freight stock exhibited featured a tar wagon, milk churn van, brake vans and open 10 ton and 12 ton wagons. The passenger station was rather uninspiringly given the name 'Newtown' and represented the then new type of pre-fabricated station building featuring a large Booking Hall and a subway connecting the platforms. A signalbox, goods shed and locomotive depot were also included demonstrating the latest type of equipment for each depot.

Over the years Pathe News filmed many of these Schoolboys' Exhibitions which had celebrated their 21st year two years before in 1948 and which was designed to appeal to boys and youths from 14 to 21 years. The exhibitions were sponsored by the *Daily Mail* and continued, with the addition of Schoolgirls in the title, into the late 1960s.

A selection of these film clips can be found on Youtube with that for 1953 for example showing the cab mock up of No. 70000 *Britannia* being eagerly explored by hordes of schoolboys kitted out in regulation blazers and caps thronging the footplate. As the narrator explains "Like most of the stands at the exhibition this one encourages every boy to become a man and every man to be a boy again."

No details were provided as to the scale of the models nor of their manufacture, although it would be reasonable to assume this was 'O' gauge and with items perhaps made by an organisation such as Bassett-Lowke.

With grateful thanks to Brian Wheeler.

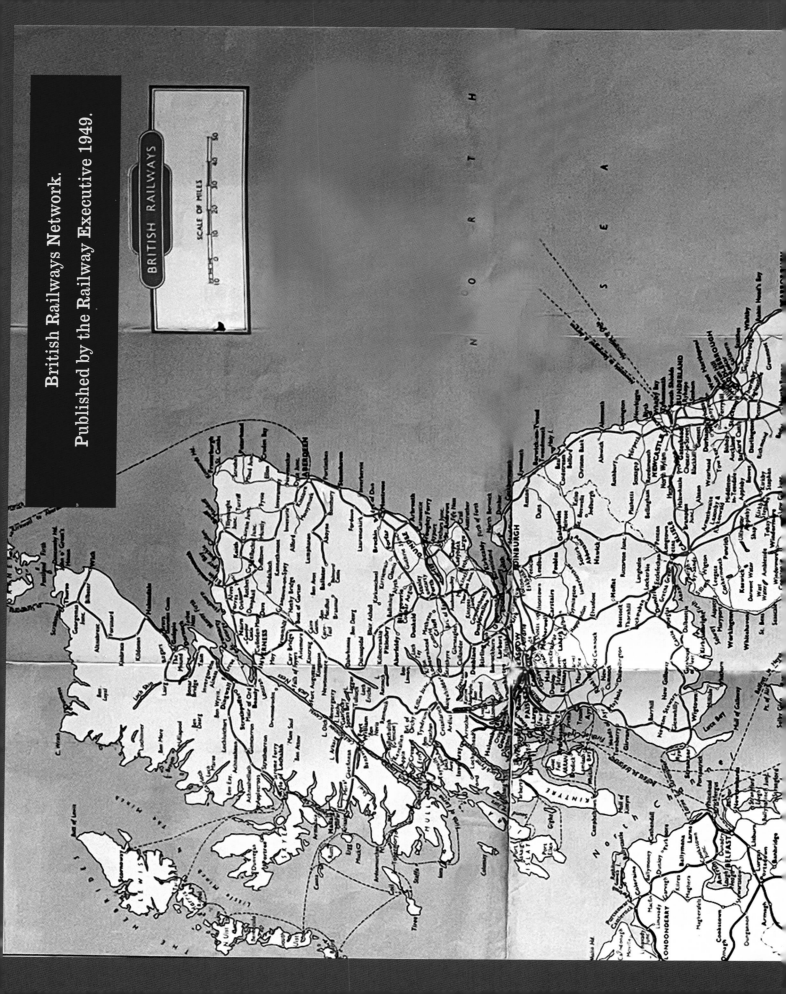

British Railways Network.

Published by the Railway Executive 1949.

BRITISH RAILWAYS

SCALE OF MILES

'4DD' - NOT SO MUCH AN 'EMU' MORE AN 'MMU' (MALODOROUS MULTIPLE UNIT).

Along with the Leader and the Tavern Car, the double deck electric multiple unit (DD) was one of Bulleid's less successful ventures.

Designed with the best intentions of carrying more people than a traditional EMU and thereby removing the need for expensive and disruptive lengthening of platforms on the busy commuter route from Charing Cross to Dartford, Nos. 4001 and 4002 were two four car units built at Eastleigh and Lancing.

Designed to run in multiple when peak loads demanded, each unit could carry 508 passengers, plus 44 accommodated in occasional tip up seats located on the upper deck, this was against the normal 4 car EMU load of 386, an increase of 31%.

Only 4½ ins. higher than normal suburban stock the way the seating was arranged was quite ingenious although on the lower deck tall passengers and those wearing some types of headgear - hats were the norm in those days – were liable to hit their heads when rising from their seats due to the overhang of the top deck seating reducing the headroom over the lower deck seating.

The floor of the upper deck is four feet higher than the usual floor and has strip lighting and curved windows that cannot be opened due to the danger of passengers leaning out at that increased height. This lack of fresh air combined with the fact that many passengers smoked cigarettes or, even worse, pipes in those days plus the body heat generated especially on hot summer days meant that the atmosphere was inclined to get rather stuffy. To combat this pressurised ventilation was installed although in practice this proved to be somewhat unreliable. Ventilation fans were mounted in plenum chambers, which also contained electric radiators

Opposite and this page bottom right - The ingenious layout of the double deck coaches is illustrated in this image although the happy smiles of passengers, posed here for publicity purposes, were not always replicated in the day to day reality of travelling in these units. The views were taken in the wooden mock-up either at Lancing or Marylebone.

Top left - Access to the upper level was via this stairway.

Top right - This view of the upper seating level shows the non opening windows and the step down to the floor level.

for heating, below the upper compartments and fresh air was drawn in from underneath the vehicle, the system being controlled by the guard. Another problem found in service was the liability of the wheels to crack after a time as they were of a smaller diameter than usual as dictated by the design of the new unit. There were some plus points however with virtually silent running and an almost complete absence of oscillation at all speeds being particularly noticeable during the trial runs. As it had been impossible to provide seating for all passengers at peak times on the Dartford lines for many years, BR felt that this route would be a useful test bed before putting the idea into full scale production.

A mock up section of a coach was exhibited at Marylebone station - a short clip of this being shunted into one of the platforms at the GC terminus is available on Youtube.

Press run for the new train.

Herbert Morrison Deputy Prime Minister and Alfred Barnes Minister of Transport travelled on a special run from Charing Cross on 1 November prior to the commencement of public services the following day.

In practice the advantage of carrying a greater number of people was outweighed by the fact that there was only one door for every 22 seats compared to one door for every 10-12 seats in a conventional unit. This resulted in delays in boarding and alighting so increasing the dwell time at each stop. This made it very difficult to maintain the timetabled service with consequent disruptive effects upon other traffic on this congested route. The upshot was that no further units of this type were built and ultimately platforms had to be lengthened at stations on the Dartford route to accommodate 10 car trains.

One of the greatest criticisms levelled by the travelling public was that passengers on the lower deck were treated to the aroma of the upper deck passengers' feet! Having said that, the units were an interesting experiment and remained the only double deck trains to run on the mainline in the UK staying in service until October 1971, by now renumbered 4901/4902, and achieving a mileage of some 700,000 during their lifetime. Two driving motor brake coaches survive (just) in preservation one owned by the Bulleid 4DD Double Deck EMU Supporters Group and one by the Northamptonshire Ironstone Railway Trust. *(Ed: They have recently been reunited for the first time in 40 years at a site at Sellindge in Kent where the Bulleid DD Society is planning to restore the coaches to museum condition for display.)*

North Pembrokeshire closure

In 1895 the North Pembrokeshire line formed part of the original route to Fishguard before the easier route from Clarbeston Road was opened in August 1906.

Having a gradient as steep as 1 in 27 for just over one mile between Clynderwen and Rosebush and being single track throughout it was always considered unsuitable for main line traffic. With the inauguration of the Fishguard – Rosslare steamer service in 1906 an alternative route was necessary and thus opened the shorter, more easily graded section from Clarbeston Road to Letterston Junction. By 1937 alternative bus services had creamed off much of the local traffic on the original route and passenger services were withdrawn although goods traffic continued. However, in 1942 the section between Puncheston and Letterston was closed completely and the former through route worked as two isolated sections - Clynderwen to Puncheston and Letterston Junction to Letterston. Whilst this latter section remains open the section from Clynderwen has been closed completely from May 1949.

Top - This view of Letterston Junction dates from May 1961, the line to the left heads for Letterston whilst that to the right is the mainline from Fishguard to Clarbeston Road. The section from Clarbeston Road to Letterston Junction was singled in the 1970s and the signalbox here closed at the same time with a ground frame operated loop retained at Letterston Junction to allow services on the Trecwn trip to run round. The goods service to Letterston not being withdrawn until March 1965 although a private siding to Trecwn remained in use for a while longer.
James Harold

Map by Ian Young.

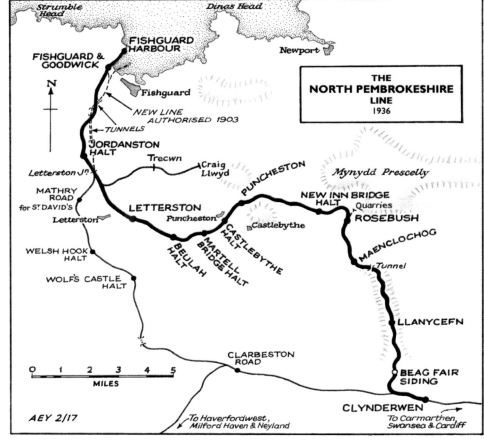

THE NORTH PEMBROKESHIRE LINE 1936

For your welfare —

BRITISH
RAILWAYS

welcome
you

*Canteens are provided at many centres, they are even
taken on to the job.*

British Railways welcomes you

From 1948 until the late 1960s BR produced a booklet designed to encourage school leavers to join the railways and to welcome new entrants. These booklets summarised what the railways did, and what jobs, training, progression, and health and social facilities were on offer to potential new recruits and those who had recently joined. In 1949 for example, and running to 48 pages illustrated with cartoons and black and white images, a number of topics were covered.

In the foreword the Chairman of the Railway Executive, Sir Eustace Missenden, welcomed new recruits thus *"When you meet, for the first time, the members of a family who are strangers to you, what a difference a good welcome makes! That is just what I want to give you – a personal, friendly welcome."* The first of the sections was entitled -

Our general policy.

This section outlined the nationalisation of the railways a year before in 1948 and summed up the policy of BR as being –

To give safe, speedy, dependable railway service at reasonable cost.
To give the staff good wages, security, and conditions as good as is reasonably possible.
To make British Railways pay their way.

All very laudable aims no doubt but history would judge how successful and for how long these aspirations were met with BR plunging into debt just six years later in 1955 which also saw a very damaging labour dispute.

Our Job

Attempting to mitigate the possible disappointment when a new recruit is initially appointed to a seemingly mundane job the text went on to explain that –

"At first sight the particular job to which you have been put may not seem to you to matter much, or make much difference to the general quality of the railway service. The seemingly trivial has its essential place in the whole and for the want of it the whole will suffer. Besides, the fact that you do your first job well will make people more inclined to give you a chance to do a second."

The regional system of BR's organisation was then explained together with the different operating departments in which a "newby" might be working. The qualities required of a new entrant were spelt out in cartoon form as below -

" *Cheerful obedience* "

To modern sensibilities these cartoons and the qualities they hoped to encourage might seem somewhat dated and one would not see many instances of 'cheerful obedience' amongst modern day new recruits one suspects.

As the public see and hear us.

The substitution of the term 'customers' for 'passengers' is not as modern as one might think for back in 1950 the booklet stated that, *"When members of the public buy a railway ticket or send their goods by rail, they are customers of British Railways. Try to treat each member of the public as you would like to be treated if you changed places. Our general behaviour and appearance counts too. Suppose a football team in a big football match ambled onto the field in untidy dress and looked as though they were saying to the spectators "I couldn't care less – what would you think? A smart looking team, clean, tidy, alert and eager for whatever the day may bring, creates a good impression before the match begins. Some of you will wear our uniform, make it look a uniform to be proud of and let people see that you are proud to wear it."*

Some interesting things on British Railways.

This section related key facts and figures such as –

Our staff total about six times as many people as the crowd at Wembley on Association Football Cup Final day.

The number of passenger journeys over our railways in a year is equal to about 20 journeys by every man, woman and child in the country.

The total miles run by our locomotives in a year would be equal to about 21,500 times round the earth.

There are about 14,000 signal boxes and the men in these boxes control more than a quarter of a million railway signals, of various types.

To keep our track in good condition, we use about a quarter of a million tons of new rails every year and about 4,000,000 new sleepers.

Our great factories for building and repairing locomotives, railway carriages and wagons, employ over 84,000 men – a big crowd if you saw them all together at a football match!

(Ed: They did seem to like their football analogies, probably on the basis that this would appeal to potential young recruits and help them visualise the scale).

How does the organisation work?

Regional structure was outlined concentrating upon the wide range of staff responsibilities such as the movement of trains and traffic, customer facing staff such as ticket collectors, goods traffic roles such as lorry drivers and those involved with keeping the track in good running order. What we would today call "back office staff" also get a mention including canteen workers, stores personnel, and rolling stock maintenance and construction staff. At the more exalted end of the staff spectrum come the chiefs of department in a region who were described as *"men of acknowledged ability, special skill in their own field of work, and carrying heavy responsibility."*

The current Railway Executive personnel were shown as –

	Responsibilities
Sir Eustace Missenden	Chairman, Publicity, Public Relations
W P Allen	Staff & Establishment, Welfare, Medical
V M Barrington-Ward	Motive Power Operations, Marine & Docks
David Blee	Commercial, Passenger, Goods, Mineral, Cartage, Continental
R A Riddles	Locomotive, Carriage, Wagon, Electrical & Road Motor Engineering, Maintenance
J C L Train	Civil Engineering, Architecture, Signalling & Telecoms Engineering
General Sir Daril Watson	Stores, Police, Estate & Rating, Civil Defence, Fire Service, Paper & Printing.

(General Watson had taken over from Field Marshall Sir

William Slim in 1949. This military connection was perhaps most famously epitomised in the later appointment of General Sir Brian Robertson as Chairman of the British Transport Commission in 1953).

There were also two part time members, **Sir Wilfred Ayre** and **Mr C Nevile,** who brought experience of outside industry and agriculture to the board but they had no departmental responsibilities. Missenden retired in January 1951 to be succeeded by John Elliot.

Your opportunity.

It is stressed that beginning in one department and staying there for some time does not preclude the new recruit later moving to something more suitable or congenial. *"If you do ask for a change, however, having made up your mind carefully what it is you want, stick to it and make good."* Obviously chopping and changing was frowned upon! Allocation to a rural location does not necessarily spoil your chances of betterment – *"many of your chances will rest with yourself."* It was the intention of BR to afford new starters larger opportunities of training and to enable further education opportunities to be opened up. New entrants were encouraged to join relevant evening classes either run by local authorities or by BR themselves. A note of caution was sounded *"Don't waste your energy by trying to do too many things in one session."* It was made clear in no uncertain terms that "*there will be no future for those who drift or rely upon age or length of service alone to carry them forward."* The cartoons below and opposite demonstrate some of those qualities required to get on in BR.

" Adaptability "

"We" and "You"

Pay, security and conditions of service were all outlined with the stated aim on pay being - *"BR wish pay to be adequate and the system of payment fair and understandable. Just*

" Keenness "

as BR are expected by the staff to pay whatever is agreed with Trade Union officials, so the staff are likewise expected to keep to the agreements.

BR wish to afford security of employment and to ensure that in special cases of misfortune there are means of help. Contributory benevolent funds are available to supplement the State Insurance scheme".

With regard to conditions of employment "Railway staff enjoy what is known as a "guaranteed week" that is to say they are protected against casual employment and against being called upon to work one or two days in the week and left high and dry on others." The need for shift working, working on public holidays and Sundays and for night work is also spelt out so that the new recruit is left in no doubt. "Saturday has to count as any other weekday in the departments handling trains and passengers. We know that there are some employments where Saturday afternoon is normally free and the fact that this cannot be so in much of the railway service has been taken into account in arriving at our rates of pay." In other words you won't be able to go to football matches every Saturday!

Holiday entitlements and privilege travel are also covered such that "all may travel at half the ordinary single fare for a return journey, a privilege which extends in the majority of cases to wives and dependent children and on three occasions/year a free ticket is granted." It is the desire of BR that office accommodation should be "adequately warmed, light and airy" and although this has already been achieved in many places the recent war has adversely affected this aim and it will take some considerable time to bring railway premises everywhere up to the required standard. Meals in canteens are provided on what is "practically a cost basis."

Sport and recreation are well catered for with "Railway Sports Clubs, Amateur Dramatic Societies, Fur and Feather societies, Boxing Clubs and what not and in many places there are playing fields, billiard rooms and recreation rooms which in some places may be used as concert halls or for amateur theatricals."

Consultation between staff and management.

The role of Works Committees and LDCs (Local Departmental Committees) are outlined. Ideas and suggestions are welcomed and rewards given if the idea is adopted or even if it is is not but shows a constructive idea.

" Ingenuity "

Staff magazines and notices.

Currently each of the former mainline railway companies continues to publish their own magazines but before long there are likely to be regional editions of a national BR magazine. Staff notices are pinned to notice boards or circulated to staff and some will require reading before commencing duty as they may affect working that day.

" *Keeping in touch* "

(Ed: I'm not sure how many new entrants these days would ask how to "procure" a staff magazine!)

Conclusion.

Let us leave the final words to the authors of the booklet –

"We work for the British public and we aim to give the best possible service. This can be given only by a concern in which the staff are happy. Your supervisor and you and all of us are in it together to make a public service of which the nation can be proud."

Don't forget, copies of many of the images from this and the previous issue are available as prints and downloads.

Liverpool Street - Shenfield electrification

September 26 1949 saw a small ceremony take place at London's Liverpool Street station when the Minister of Transport, Alfred Barnes, cut a ribbon to inaugurate the completion of the electrification scheme to Shenfield.

A special train carrying the distinguished guests left the terminus at 11am calling at several stations en route to Shenfield subsequently returning non-stop to London whilst normal services would commence the following day.

Although the scheme was originally authorised back in 1936, with work starting in 1937, like many another project it was brought to a halt in 1940 by WW2 when many 'doodlebugs' damaged large parts of the east end. The scheme designed to reduce congestion in this part of the capital was in two parts, the first being the electrification of LNER lines from Liverpool Street to Shenfield and from Fenchurch Street to Stratford which was costed at £3.5m. Secondly, as part of the New Works programme for 1935 to improve the capital's transport infrastructure, an extension of the LT Central Line from Liverpool Street to Stratford and Leyton and then its projection over LNER lines to Loughton and Ongar and to Newbury Park via Hainault was proposed together with the construction of a new Underground line from Newbury Park to Leytonstone.

The majority of this second element was completed by 1948, with the extension of the tube network to Epping following in September 1949, which allowed steam worked services between Liverpool Street and Hainault to be withdrawn thus allowing the provision of more paths through the congested Liverpool Street to Stratford section for a frequent electric service.

1500 volts DC supplied from overhead wires was the chosen system over the four track 25 route mile section affected and some heavy civil engineering works have been required such as the provision of a flyover, brought into service in October 1947, between Manor Park and Ilford to carry the up and down local lines over the through lines thus securing electric services an uninterrupted path into Liverpool Street. Stratford station has been remodelled with additional platforms and tracks to accommodate the Central Line tube trains and to facilitate passenger interchange. A station at Crowland Heath situated between Romford and Chadwell Heath has not in the end been provided as the surrounding area now lies in the Green Belt.

Over thirty mechanical signal boxes have been replaced by three modernised existing boxes and nine new all electric boxes which operate the 'route system' whereby the signalman merely actuates a route switch which sets the

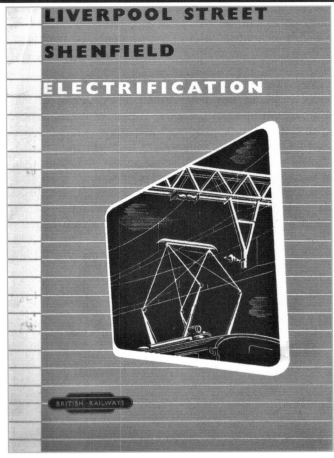

desired route and clears the relative signals as soon as the route is available thus removing the need for the physical movement of signals and point levers. Four aspect colour light signalling has been installed with continuous track circuiting between Liverpool Street and Gidea Park which should permit a theoretical 1½ min heasdway between trains. Colour lights and track circuiting are already in place between Gidea Park and Chelmsford / Southend thus completing one of the longest continuous sections of colour light signalling on BR. All signals are equipped with telephones to enable drivers to communicate with signalmen in the event of problems. Six electricity sub stations have been erected and a continuously manned control centre has been established at Chadwell Heath.

Ninety two 3-coach units, consisting of a motor coach, a trailer and a driving trailer, have been supplied running in 9-car formations during peak hours and capable of carrying 1,224 passengers but only 43% of whom will be seated. Birmingham Railway Carriage & Wagon Co. built the driving trailers and Metropolitan-Cammell built all other cars. Two pairs of sliding doors per coach are fitted with buttons provided for the opening of individual doors by passengers but closure of all doors is under the guard's control. A five lamp route indicator is positioned below the offside window on the driving units. The intermediate trailers were intended to have both first and third class accommodation provided but the Ministry of War Transport had abolished all first class transport on suburban London services in 1941 thus the trailers were built with only third class provision.

Ilford houses a new depot for the cleaning, repair and maintenance of the stock together with a carriage washing plant. The 38 daily new electric services will initially run in steam timings but from November accelerated schedules to an increased frequency will operate and finally next spring some 21 trains / hour will run during the peak periods reaching Shenfield in 33 minutes, saving 13 minutes on the former steam timings, having called only at Romford and then all intermediate stations. *(Ed: The final unit initially classified AM6 then later Class 306 was withdrawn in 1981, one car has been preserved at Shildon Locomotive Museum).*

Traffic levels rose by almost 50% during the first year of electric operation – a striking example of the 'Sparks Effect'.

Electric unit No.14 leading with a down Southend service at Bethnal Green on 28 February 1959. Judging by the heaps of bricks and sand on the platform of the station some extensive building work was in progress here. *R C Riley*

End of the road for three 'Premier Line' stalwarts

April – June 1949 saw the withdrawal of the last active members of three famous L&NWR classes - the Claughton, Prince of Wales and Precursor.

CLAUGHTON 4-6-0

With the withdrawal of LMS No.6004 which had been allocated a BR number that it had never received and that was formerly named *Princess Louise* although this had been removed in June 1935, the last of the 'Claughtons' was retired in April 1949 having travelled some 893,000 miles in service since completion in 1920. Some 130 examples were built to the design of Charles Bowen-Cooke between 1913 –

1921 the doyen of the class being named after the Chairman of the L&NWR Sir Gilbert Claughton. They worked express passenger services for a number of years and received modifications such as Caprotti valve gear and modified boilers but the introduction of the Royal Scot class in 1927 saw much of the Claughton's mainline work removed and by 1937 just a quartet remained in service Nos. 5946, 6004, 6017 and 6023. Three went in 1940/41 leaving just No. 6004 to soldier on mainly hauling freight trains between London and Liverpool's Edge Hill yard becoming increasingly decrepit and careworn as the years went by. When BR inherited this sole survivor in 1948 it was allocated No. 46004 but, as stated, this was never carried.

Right - LMS Claughton Class No. 5906 named *Ralph Brocklebank* is seen on shed. Constructed in 1913 this locomotive was withdrawn in 1937. *R C Riley*

Bottom - On 24 April 1949 No. 6004, last of the line, was on the scrap line at Crewe awaiting its fate. *Transport Library*

On 12 July 1935 No. 5972 gets away from Penrith. This was one of the class fitted with a larger boiler from 1928. It was to last in traffic until May 1937. *Transport Library*

PRINCE OF WALES 4-6-0

Between 1911-24, 246 locomotives of this class designed by Bowen-Cooke were constructed, the majority at Crewe but 20 were built by the North British Locomotive Co. and 91 by the Glasgow based firm of William Beardmore & Co.

Although Joy's valve gear was fitted to the vast majority four existing locomotives together with the final one built were given Walschaerts gear. The investiture of Prince Edward, the future Edward VIII, as Prince of Wales in 1911 provided the spur to name the first of the class. Introduced in 1934 Black Fives displaced most of them on passenger duties and by 1939 just 22 remained in service with BR inheriting the last six members in 1948. The final quartet were allocated BR numbers 58000-3 but none received them before withdrawal. Withdrawn in May 1949 the final example No. 25752 completed 855,000 miles in service.

Prince of Wales Class sporting LMS No. 25787 was built in October 1921 and was to last until withdrawal in May 1948. *Neville Stead*

No. 25683. Originally named *Falaba*, is seen on shed in the company of more modern motive power in the shape of a Black Five. This Prince of Wales class locomotive was withdrawn in January 1946 and was named in commemoration of the Falaba a passenger ship of the Elder Dempster Line. She left Liverpool for Sierra Leone on 27 March 1915 and sighted the German submarine U-28 off the southern coast of Ireland the following day. U-28 surfaced, sent two warnings and Falaba's crew were ordered to abandon ship. As the final lifeboat was being lowered, a torpedo hit and 104 lives were lost. *Neville Stead*

Still with its LMS No. 25752 this was the last of the class to be withdrawn in June 1949 from Stafford shed. *Neville Stead*

PRECURSOR 4-4-0

Introduced by George Whale, locomotive superintendent of the L&NWR, between 1904-07, 130 examples were constructed at Crewe. As originally built, they were saturated, though some were later superheated. They were later developed by Bowen-Cooke into the superheated 'George V' class. Withdrawals of the saturated locomotives began in 1927 with the last example of an as-built locomotive going in 1935. Withdrawals of the superheated locomotives began in 1935 and by the outbreak of WW2 only seven survived with BR inheriting a single example in No. 25297 *Sirocco* which was withdrawn in June 1949 after having run nearly 1.5m miles.

Happier times. No 5315 *Delamere* at Euston. This engine had a working life of just 29 years and had been withdrawn in 1936.
R C Riley

Photographed on 29 May 1949, shortly before withdrawal the following month, the last Precursor No. 25297 formerly named *Sirocco* is seen in the twilight of its career. Although allocated the BR number 58010 this was never carried. *Neville Stead*

Ex-LNWR 3P 4-4-0 Precursor class No 25319 *Bucephalus* is seen standing at Platform 1, Coventry Station, on an up passenger service on 16 February 1939. Built as LNWR No 990 in April 1906 it gained its LMS running number - No 5319 - in July 1927 and was later placed on the duplicate list by adding the number '2' prefix to its number. It was withdrawn in December 1940 and was scrapped at Crewe works immediately afterwards. The train is a Birmingham to Rugby or Leamington Spa working which probably goes forward to Euston via Northampton. The wisp of steam from the cab roof is coming from the carriage warming safety valve - a rarely seen phenomenon. Steam at the front end and beneath the first coach shows that the crew have steam heat on -it was obviously a very cold day. The first coach is a MR suburban brake third. © *David P Williams Colour Archive; Original photograph by Harry W Robinson.*

New Diesel Shunters for the Southern Region

Ashford Works have recently completed the first of a batch of 15, 350hp 0-6-0 diesel shunters, ordered by the Southern Railway before nationalisation, designed for non hump yard shunting and light transfer duties. Initially they will be based at Norwood Junction and Hither Green shed for local yard shunting duties.

Numbered 15211-25 they were designed by Bulleid with his larger BFB disc wheels and can reach a maximum speed of 27 ½ mph somewhat higher than the normal diesel shunter. Weighing in at 49 tons and with a tractive effort of 24,000 lb., the power unit comprised a six cylinder four stroke English Electric diesel engine coupled to a six pole 190kw DC generator. Two axle hung suspended traction motors, one on each of the outer axles, drive through a 17.5 : 1 double reduction gear.

They were provided with a central dual controlled desk but in order to start the engine oil had first to be pumped up to engage the pressure switch. However as the pump was in the engine compartment this meant that starting required the services of two people, one pumping and the

Doyen of the experimental trio of new diesel shunters designed by Maunsell, No. 15201, is seen on shed at Eastleigh on 23 September 1963 keeping company with rebuilt Bulleid pacific No. 34009 *Padstow.*

In June 1961 Norwood Junction shed played host to No. 15203 the third of the first trio of diesel shunters and Class C2X No. 32545 which would be withdrawn at the end of that year. *Jack A C Kirke*

other on the control handle engaging the start position. Maintenance was relatively easy with the exhaust valves being located in cages which could be extracted without removal of the cylinder head as was the case on other types of diesel shunter.

They formed the second batch of 0-6-0 diesel shunters ordered by the SR with the first experimental trio, 15201-

3, being designed by Maunsell in 1937. Further examples of Bulleid's design were built between 1949-52 being numbered 15226-36. *(Ed: the class was withdrawn between 1968-71 and one survives after having been sold by BR to the National Coal Board for use in the Kent coalfield and is currently on the Spa Valley Railway)*

Above - No. 15225 seen at Gillingham shed on 15 April 1956 was one of the new breed of shunter designed by Bulleid. *Roy WIlson*

Opposite top - One of the final batch of 0-6-0 diesel shunters No. 15227 is seen outside Hither Green shed on 25 April 1953. *Arthur Carpenter*

Opposite bottom - Seen from the rear, the cab overhang and cut out section at the back of the locomotive thus aiding rear visibility whilst shunting is very evident in this view of No. 15203 at Norwood Junction on 6 November 1964.

British Transport Films (BTF)

Announced in January and established in May 1949 the Films Section of the BTC was charged with the production of documentary films, either made in house or through contracting out, for general exhibition. They were to be of an instructional nature for staff and to inform and educate the general public about the new nationalised transport industries of the country. Film making on the railways had had a long history with the LMS, the Southern Railway and London Transport all having their own dedicated units producing such films as that featuring the *Royal Scot* on its 1933 USA tour. So popular did this newsreel film prove that the LMS converted an old coach into a mobile cinema which toured customers and staff in the LMS territory showing films which enhanced and promoted the company's image. Other companies such as the GPO also had their own film units producing such classics as 'Night Mail' in 1936.

Picking up on this idea the BTC appreciated the importance of having its own film unit to record not just railway but road, dock and inland waterway transport stories within its own nationalised empire. Placed in charge of this new unit was renowned documentary film maker Edgar Anstey who was a protégée of film pioneer John Grierson who was credited with coining the term 'documentary' to describe films which were factual and thought provoking and who in 1928 had produced the film entitled 'Drifters' about the Scottish fishing industry which is still hailed today as a landmark of the genre.

Anstey was appointed producer in charge of BTF in May 1949 and promptly got to work setting up the new unit recruiting a team of 30 full time in-house professionals including cameramen, editors, writers and technicians. This team, with occasional outside help to compose music for specific film scores, went on to complete some 700 productions over the next 37 years until the final film released in 1986. Anstey's brief was to produce films which trumpeted the virtues of the country's newly nationalised transport industries thereby encouraging the public to use their facilities whilst at the same time providing information to assist in training the staff of those industries. By the end of 1949 four films had been completed ready for showing the following year, these were –

"Mr Arnot of Waverley station
Has a very high sense of occasion
When the train's a non-stopper
His Topper is proper
His Homberg's for trains of low station".

Transport – described the development, achievements, aims and organisation of British transport. This would be taken up by Pathe Pictures for a wide theatrical distribution.

Berth 24 – described the turnaround of a ship at Hull docks

Moving House – made by Public Relations Films for the BTF showed how the capable hands of British Road services staff could handle the daunting task of moving a family

Inland Waterways – a staff information film for circulation within the Docks & Inland Waterways Executive and to show to other parts of the BTC workforce how one group of British transport workers did their job

The film unit would go on to produce many classics of railway interest over the years including –

Farmer Moving South 1952
Elizabethan Express 1954
Snowdrift at Bleath Gill 1955
Blue Pullman 1960
Terminus 1961 directed by John Schlesinger
John Betjeman goes by train 1962
Snow 1963 – received several major awards upon release and was nominated for a BAFTA award in 1964 and an Academy Award in 1966
Railways Forever 1970

Self-Weighing tenders

Following the conclusion of trials on the London Midland Region BR decided to equip nine locomotives with coal-weighing apparatus in their tenders.

This consisted of a separate vertical sided bunker with self-trimming back which was located inside the tender being normally locked into position on brackets when the locomotive was moving. When the coal is to be weighed the locks are released and the load is transmitted by a system of levers to a steelyard on which, by means of the rather Heath Robinson method of sliding weights, the amount could be measured, the readings being taken from equipment located in a padlocked cabinet at the rear of the bunker. The tenders so equipped will be moved around between different locomotive types in order to test a variety of motive power. The overall aim is to establish coal consumption, using differing grades and types of coal, whilst locomotives are engaged in the same tasks over a given section of route. Shunting, shed work, standing idle and train working will all be encompassed by the trials and the results of differing firing and driving practices upon coal consumption can be demonstrated to footplate crew with the aim of achieving the most economical methods of working. They can be used either alone or in conjunction with a dynamometer car if required.

Several Black 5s were so equipped including Nos. 44677, 45298, 44697, 44971 and 44986 and on the Eastern region four self-weighing tenders were attached at times to B1 and K1 class members including No. 61095.

Castle class No. 7018 carried one on the Western region and the Southern region's only example, tender No. 3343, was attached to a variety of Merchant Navy pacifics beginning with No. 35018 in June 1952 and afterwards to Nos. 35014, 35015 and 35024. The equipment was removed from the Southern region tender in December 1961. Over time many fell into disuse and the bunkers were fixed, steelyards removed and they continued in service as normal tenders for many years until the locomotive's withdrawal.

Opposite top - This view of Class B1 No. 61095 B1 shows the self-weighing tender at an unidentified depot coaling plant. *Eric Sawford*

Opposite bottom - Black Five No. 45298 with its self weighting tender in tow passes Bangor No. 2 signalbox. *Ken Nutall*

Above - This rear view of B1 Class No. 61140 at Glasgow Eastfield shed on 10 April 1954 gives a good illustration of the modifications necessitated by the fitting of a self weighing tender. *W A C Smith*

Brief Encounters

RAILWAY CATERING

Nine months after taking over control in July 1948 of all refreshment rooms, of which there were 400 working and 31 non functioning ones, except on the Southern Region where private management still retain some contracts, the Hotels Executive of the BTC have had a chance to review the prices, profits and losses from various catering services.

Restoration of buffet/restaurant car services to pre war levels saw some 500 regular weekday trains offering such facilities. However the 4/- meal sold on trains for example would have resulted in a 5½d loss were it not for the profit of 8d made on accompanying beverages. A breakdown of the 4/- charged reveals that 2/0½d is spent on wages, 3d on repairs, maintenance, furniture and utensils, 3d on fuel and light and 3d on insurance, laundry, uniforms etc. This leaves a sum of just 1/2½d to be spent on the food which in fact costs 1/8d thus leading to the loss mentioned above. This 1/8d cost relating to the provision of cod or sausages rises to 1/10d for turbot, 2/- for halibut, 2/10d for salmon or a staggering 3/2d for chicken. *(Ed: chicken more expensive than turbot – not at today's prices I feel).*

When it comes to beverages tea, of which there are 40 million cups served annually, is charged at 3d a cup of which half is absorbed by the cost of replacing lost or damaged crockery there being 5 million breakages annually. Apparently a replacement cup and saucer sourced from Poland or Czechoslovakia costs 1/-. The Railway Executive has decided to reduce this loss by serving tea in moulded paper cups with handles. Additionally, following successful trials in the North Eastern region, it has been decided that on some services trolleys, no more than 9¼ ins. wide being specially designed to negotiate coach corridors, will be employed, one containing eatables and the other non alcoholic drinks, serving passengers in their compartments thus avoiding much of the carrying of trays which currently occupies restaurant car staff. Luncheon boxes priced at 2/- or 3/- have also been introduced.

Top - Class distinctions still applied when this image of a Second Class Refreshment Room sign was taken at an unidentified location. *Mike Pescod*

Right - This view of the interior of a Mk I Buffet Car was taken at an exhibition to gauge public reaction. *British Railways*

WHOSE A PRETTY BOY THEN?

The LMR have plans to transport some 5 million pigeons during the coming season which runs from April to September now that restrictions placed upon the carriage of such traffic in 1938 have been lifted. In addition to the birds carried dedicated pigeon specials will accommodate 'Pigeon Convoyers' who are engaged by the various pigeon racing clubs to feed and water the birds whilst en route and to release them at their destination. Specials already arranged by the LMR include four train loads of Irish racing pigeons travelling from Heysham to Penzance, Bude and Milford Haven in June.

'Up up and away'. Two views of pigeon releases from railway vans, the first image being taken at Selby with the second image located at Winchester.

ENVIRONMENTALLY AWARE

651 stations have entered this year's 'Best Kept Station Competition' organised by the LMR. Judges will make two surprise visits to stations, one in the summer and one in the winter, points being awarded for flower and shrub cultivation, cleanliness of waiting rooms and platforms, and neatness of posters and timetables. Allowance will be made for those stations without gardens or those situated in industrial or blitzed areas in order that they will not feel disadvantaged by their local environment.

The practice of speeding up the inspection process adopted in 1930 by fixing a seat to the front buffer beam of Holden 2-4-0 No. 7490 to accommodate the judges as they toured the southern area of the LNER will not apparently be repeated. This expedient was adopted to save time as some of the London area stations could muster only a few flowers in tubs thus warranting only a brief look by the judges. The locomotive ran light engine in most cases although in some more remote locations a saloon was attached. It is reassuring to learn that speed was limited when the judges rode the buffer beam and that no fatalities were suffered. *(Ed: Apoplexy for future Health & Safety staff no doubt!)*

Top - The station gardens at Beverley get some admiring glances. *Transport Treasury*

Left - When life was lived at a slower pace there was always plenty of time to achieve some spectacular results as this garden at an unidentified station testifies. *Transport Treasury*

Right - Barnby Dun was a small station on the line between Doncaster and Thorne and here the Station Master admires the blooms. *Transport Treasury*

PLUS ÇA CHANGE ! - DAWLISH AVOIDING LINE

Since coming to prominence in 2014 with the dramatic collapse of part of the sea wall which left track suspended in mid air and which closed the only rail route to the south west for two months, thoughts have again been turning to the provision of an alternative inland route from Exeter to Newton Abbot although future proofing the existing coastal route has for the moment taken precedence.

Prior to WW2 the GWR was also focussed on the possible provision of an inland route between Exminster and Bishopsteignton not only to provide an alternative to the coastal section but as part of their plans to quadruple the tracks between Exeter and Newton Abbot which at that time was felt to be desirable. Quadrupling of the existing coastal line was considered impracticable hence attention was directed towards a double track inland diversion. Three different routes of varying length were proposed over the years however, on 1 December 1949 BR announced that owing to 'present day circumstances' the scheme was not going ahead as the cost, estimated by then to be £18m could not be countenanced in view of the country's dire economic position.

The GWR had even gone as far as obtaining a parliamentary act to proceed with construction and surveyors' poles had appeared along the proposed route in the spring of 1939. Several properties had been acquired and some residents had vacated their homes. At least one business was needlessly wound up as the attached letter giving a reference for an employee shows. *(Ed: Seventy years on no alternative inland route has been forthcoming and so far £80m has been spent in providing a new sea wall in the Dawlish area as part of a resilience project estimated at £155m).*

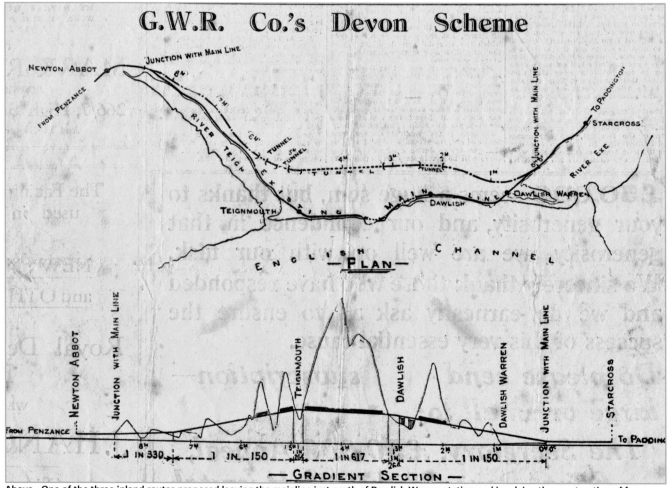

Above - One of the three inland routes proposed leaving the mainline just north of Dawlish Warren station and involving the construction of four tunnels. The other two alternative routes suggested started from Powderham and from Exminster respectively.

Opposite top - Letter from 'Porprietor' (sic) of the Teignmouth Horticultural Co.

Opposite bottom - Section of new inland route in the area of the Horticultural Nursery. *Images courtesy of Bishopsteignton Heritage Trust*

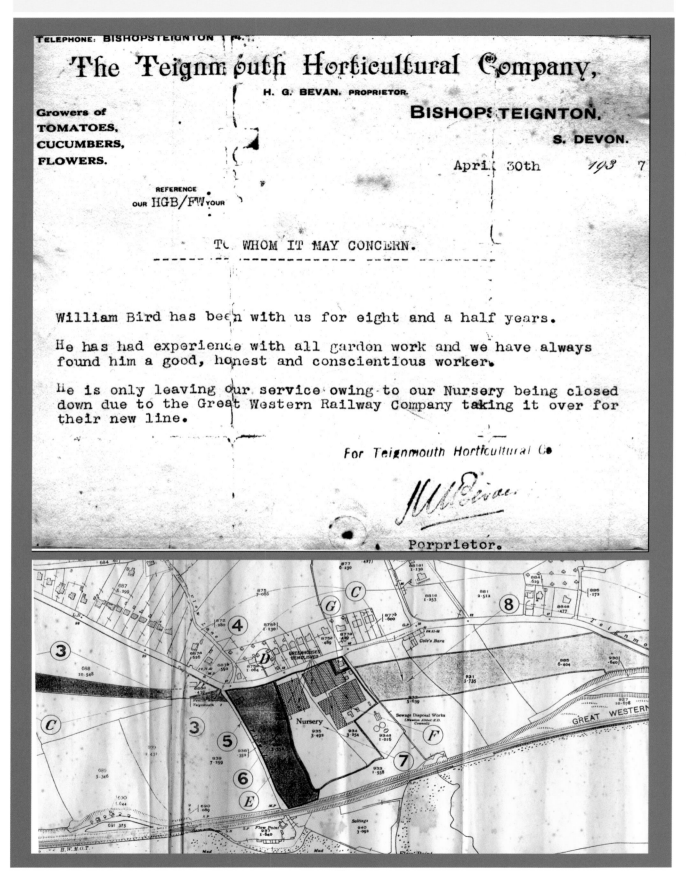

TELEPHONE: BISHOPSTEIGNTON 14.

The Teignmouth Horticultural Company,

H. G. BEVAN. PROPRIETOR.

Growers of
TOMATOES.
CUCUMBERS,
FLOWERS.

BISHOPSTEIGNTON,

S. DEVON.

April 30th 193 7

REFERENCE
OUR HGB/FW YOUR

TO WHOM IT MAY CONCERN.

William Bird has been with us for eight and a half years.

He has had experience with all garden work and we have always found him a good, honest and conscientious worker.

He is only leaving our service owing to our Nursery being closed down due to the Great Western Railway Company taking it over for their new line.

For Teignmouth Horticultural Co

Porprietor.

The Leader in 1949 - trials and tribulations

When Mr Bulleid's revolutionary steam engine design the 'Leader' first took to the rails in the last week of June 1949 there were probably some mixed emotions amongst the design team staff at Brighton.

Mixed, in the sense that there were undoubtedly some who fervently wished the concept to succeed. These were the men who had been involved in the project from the start and who perhaps saw it as a means to show that the Southern, seen by some as essentially an 'electric' railway, was one which could produce a steam design that was so revolutionary and so radical that their involvement would forever be remembered.

Conversely there were also those who were now fearful for their own careers under British Railways and who, well aware of the reputation of their chief Mr Bulleid, were less keen to fully support a design which contained so many radical aspects. It would take the failure of only one of those

innovations to possibly bring into question their own work and abilities.

Bulleid as we know was a maverick. A genius in many respects but one who on occasion really needed a steadying hand in order to achieve greatness. So was this his final UK steam design to be the work of genius, a vision capable of great achievement and one which could point towards a renaissance for steam?

The new British Railways regime was already 18 month old and so far as motive power was concerned matters were now firmly in the hand of the 'gang of three', Messrs Riddles, Cox and Bond, who were already working on a range of standard steam designs to act as a stop-gap until more modern motive power became not just available but could be afforded by the nation.

These standard designs were meant to follow basic

Raising steam No. 36001 is captured 'resting' at Dormans. This is a colourised view by David Williams from an original taken by Harry Attwell of the Testing Section at Brighton. The date is possibly 5 September 1949 and if so it records the first attempt to reach Victoria with a trailing load of 260 tons. No. 1 end is leading. The train crew comprises at least 10 people (one on the top of the bunker) including the photographer and possibly even more as there is no obvious driver and fireman (there may be two more from shadows on the ground). No. 36001 still has the front oscillating gear in place although the dust cover has been removed. In addition two vertical 'markers' have been attached to the buffer beam these being provided in an attempt to measure the degree of movement of the reciprocal motion and sleeves relative to known parameters – presumably by observation once some of the cab floorboards had been removed. It was not successful and the 'markers' were later removed.

principles, cheap and easy to build and to maintain and, whilst we cannot say with certainty, it is most likely that the basic design ideals had been set from an early stage with probably very little input from the results of the 1948 interchange trials (See item on page 17). Bulleid's pacifics had been part of these trials but there is not much evidence to indicate that Bulleid's originality could be found in the later standard range.

In order to uphold the designer's beliefs, Leader would not only have to work from the outset but also to operate fault free to have any chance of influencing steam design in the future. Time was thus of the essence.

Having been released from Brighton works No 36001 as she was designated, was handed over to the Brighton Testing Section who would oversee what would initially be light engine followed by load trials. These trials would also serve to run in the locomotive and whilst no anticipated date for entering service has been found it would be reasonable to state this was probably anticipated to be weeks rather than months into the future. As it was Leader would never achieve a single penny in revenue for its owners, the nation – 'the British tax payer' - and instead it would continue to be a drain on the nation's purse throughout its existence.

It might appear from the foregoing that we have therefore closed the story before it has hardly begun. In reality there is no harm in doing this as the history of No 36001 and how it fared is known to almost all followers of railway history even if some of the detail that created that failure is perhaps not so familiar. Consequently we may perhaps start, almost the way we mean to go on, and report that the very first trial run on 22 June 1949 was not a success when the engine disgraced itself by failing to reverse out of Brighton station after the short journey from the works to the running shed and as a result it was towed back into works for attention.

It was back on the rails again, this time with more success, three days later and accompanied by a tank locomotive no doubt for 'insurance' as the traffic department could not afford to have the new locomotive fail on the main line with the consequent delays to other traffic. All though was well and the next day No 36001 travelled to Eastleigh, again with an 'insurance' locomotive.

At Eastleigh No 36001 was inspected by those who were, or thought they were, important and it was paraded up and down the works yard to appropriate admiring glances. Whether such congratulations and admiration was superficial it is difficult to say but in reality probably yes as those present were either the remnants of the old guard from the 'Big-Four' most of whom were due be turned out to pasture if they had not already been, or who were following the new regime and thus supportive of what was to come.

Bulleid was there of course but otherwise the men at the actual works were kept strictly away although this did not prevent one curious young apprentice from venturing out when he thought the coast was clear only to unexpectedly meet Bulleid himself. Years later that same apprentice would recall how, fearful of chastisement, he was instead met with the opposite being allowed free rein to explore the new design subject to being asked for his opinion afterwards which turned out to be positive – naturally!

Confidence was thus high as No 36001 had not required the benefits of its back up locomotives either locally at Brighton or en-route to Eastleigh. Festivities over she therefore set off alone to return to Brighton for the start of her trials. Now though her reliability, or rather lack of it, would begin to show through for out of 17 days running starting with the return from Eastleigh through to the 31 August on no less than 10 days of failures were recorded.

Under such circumstances it might be expected that perhaps a single aspect of the unconventional design was at fault but recall Leader had several major design differences compared to a conventional steam design, namely the offset boiler, sleeve valves, dry-back (no water jacket) firebox and it was all of these that in the event gave trouble. In addition there were lubrication and reversing gear issues, the irony being that a component might work perfectly for a week and then fail seemingly for no obvious reason. One example during 1949 was when Bulleid himself was on the locomotive and gave instructions for it to be worked flat out for a period with words akin to,'...Let us get to the top of this climb as quickly as possible....then if something is going to break it will surely happen'. They did get to the top and - nothing went amiss. On this particular day Bulleid left the engine at lunchtime and the crew repeated the route that same afternoon – whether with the same gusto is not reported – but in the absence of the maestro the inevitable occurred - the locomotive failed. Aside from the first two day's running and perhaps tempting fate all the trials so far had been solo efforts with no 'insurance' provided. With hindsight this might appear strange but cost and manpower availability were probable reasons.

Having reported the negative perhaps we should redress the balance and try to accentuate the positive and by 2 September 1949 the engine had achieved four days of (reported) fault-free running and it was decided to attempt a load trial and not just any load trial either but one that would take the engine from Brighton to Victoria.

Reading between the lines it is almost certain this was Bulleid needing to prove to others, and perhaps even convince himself, that his design was viable. Having it successfully work into Victoria would be his vindication. Maybe he was already wary that Messrs Riddles & Co. might cancel the whole project at the stroke of a pen – they almost did just two months later when, having received reports of the poor showing of the prototype, work was ordered to be stopped on the remaining engines then under construction. It would never resume.

So back to 5 September and Leader set off running initially east from Brighton via Lewes and then north towards Oxted. More difficulties ensued on the way and having run short of steam and then pausing for a 'blow-up' or crawling along at reduced speed, the decision was taken to terminate the test run at Oxted.

At this point the reader might well ask why once sufficient steam pressure had been recovered did they not simply carry on? We may assume Bulleid was perhaps on the engine as well. Whatever the reason any good that Leader might have done to confirm its reputation by arriving in London would have been more than undone had it failed there and held up other traffic in the process. Ironically it was on Victoria to Oxted line services as well as on through trains between Brighton and Bournemouth that Leader had been proposed to work once it entered traffic.

A second attempt was made three days later but again with the same result. On this occasion it came closer to achieving its goal but this time the attempt was scuppered for political reasons. Initially it ran well but things started to go awry although not before one individual at Brighton knowing the engine was on its way to London contacted a colleague at 222 Marylebone Road with words to the effect that if he wished to see Leader in London he had better get across to Victoria quickly. Unfortunately said conversation was overheard by Col. Harold Rudguard the BRB member for motive power. Folklore has it that it was then Rudguard who immediately got hold of Southern control and told them in no uncertain terms that the locomotive was not to continue. By this time it was struggling anyway and thus Leader's opportunity to reach London was over. (Two of the class did come to London later, that is if we may count New Cross shed as London, but they were towed out of steam during the period the project was in limbo awaiting a decision. With the concept later cancelled they were towed back south again and subsequently scrapped at Brighton.)

The next six weeks or so, from 16 September to 31 October witnessed 19 days of test runs mostly with loads varying between 150 and 255 tons the actual weight behind the drawbar consisting of whatever stock was available but it was always passenger never goods vehicles. Only on six days did the locomotive achieve anything like success and as before this was due to a variety of reasons although the main difficulties did now seem to centre on the firebox brick lining and the cylinder oscillating gear; the latter affixed to the front of the cylinders and intended to assist in lubricating

the sleeves and so prevent 'dry' areas. To effect a hoped for cure, an additional layer of firebricks on the inside and rear of the dry sides was added whilst the reciprocating gear was removed first from one bogie and then from the other. Both had the desired effect and, taking November 1949 as a whole, the locomotive was active for 16 days with just four failures recorded. Even so it could hardly be considered a resounding success and Leader was certainly not yet reliable enough for revenue earning service. Whether any consideration was given to attempting such workings is not reported but we may probably say unlikely. It was also in November that the decree came down from on high at Marylebone to postpone work on the other four examples of the five that had been ordered. The signs were ominous.

There were just nine outings in December, mostly successful but two not so. Time was also running out for the locomotive at Brighton. The Chief Civil Engineer had received a report citing concerns of track spreading on the reverse curves between Brighton and Lewes. *(See Southern Times No 4).* For the past 70+ years such stories had been little more than folklore, an allegation made but without proof. That all changed in 2022 when a file of papers surfaced that finally proved the point and with the added rider that Leader often exceeded its stipulated 50mph maximum on this section of line.

Unequal weight distribution was considered one of the causes hence the last outing of No 36001 in 1949, on 16 December, was light to Eastleigh and return for weighing.

Ironically the engine behaved perfectly in both directions but not on the weigh table at Eastleigh with an imbalance of several tons on one side compared with the other being revealed. Stephen Townroe, then the Assistant District Motive Power Superintendent at Eastleigh, witnessed the event and recounted later how the dials on one side went off the scale at their maximum of 30 tons. Leader's fate, at Brighton at least, was thus sealed. It returned in disgrace to Brighton and where for reasons, officially at least, citing the demands of the peak Christmas traffic and lack of crews, it was quietly laid up for several weeks.

We may briefly stray here into the new year – 1950. Riddles could well have been expected to cancel the testing and scrap the project but instead the locomotive was to be transferred for further trials at Eastleigh. It was at Eastleigh that it would achieve its greatest success but before this came to pass also its greatest failure. Sadly it was the latter debacle that would be officially remembered and the project was inevitably cancelled in early 1951.

So had Bulleid's work been wasted, had Riddles killed off a viable design? Here we must look at the facts and not consider the emotion. It is a truism that it is through innovation in engineering that advancements are made. Bulleid believed he could make a difference and provide a future, or at least a longer term future for steam, but Leader was not to be the way forward. In this country the LMS and its successor the London Midland region were already experimenting with diesel-electric power. The Southern region would follow suit very shortly and the Western region were innovating with Gas Turbine propulsion. All BR regions were similarly 'tinkering' with steam ideas as it was the conventional steam engine that continued to provide the principal motive power on the system.

If there was someone, somewhere, who was progressing steam design it was Andre Chapelon in France. Concurrent with the development of Leader Chapelon was rebuilding a huge 4-6-4 tender engine which size for size was destined to be more efficient and produce more power than any steam engine ever built before. Undoubtedly Bulleid wished to leave his mark, which he did, but perhaps for the wrong reasons. Too late now but perhaps importing some of the French ideas might have been the way forward.

Kevin Robertson

The comic opera. At Oxted Harry Attwell was on board to record this unique moment. The water filler on Leader was on the top of the locomotive and nobody seems to have initially considered that the water columns on the SR's Central section would not reach. Improvisation was required and Brighton fashioned a form of copper chute and extended leather bag. Very much a 'Heath-Robinson' arrangement it nevertheless worked after a fashion – the disadvantage being that taking water could mean an hour's delay (and a soaking!). The adaptor was carried on the engine for the trials originating from Brighton - although on at least one occasion it was forgotten. No water - test cancelled. The height of the Mogul tender alongside forms a useful comparison. (Access to the tank top was via a set of steps on the rear end of the tank in No. 2 cab and then through the cab roof vent.)

Another Oxted view with the test train waiting to head back towards Brighton. Observe the driver (?) standing at the cab door and from his position it is apparent that he is clearly foul of the loading gauge. Of necessity during shunt movements the cab door had to be open but if he looked outside he risked being dangerously close to lineside structures. *J G Click / National Railway Museum*

Barry Railway 0-6-0T finale

The final example of a Barry Railway 0-6-0T locomotive No. 784, ex Barry Railway No. 51, was withdrawn in August. It retained its original boiler and distinctive capuchon chimney until the very end.

One of five examples built between 1889-91 by Hudswell Clark, it entered service in 1890 with one No. 783 lasting until withdrawal in August 1948 whilst No. 784 soldiered on until August this year. They were designed by Hosgood for light shunting duties at docks and their diminutive size made them particularly suited to shunting on the breakwater at Barry Island. Access to this breakwater was via a very roughly hewn tunnel which had sharp curves and limited clearance making it impossible for other locomotives of the company to negotiate the bore. After their initial use as shunting locomotives they also took on certain passenger duties on the Vale of Glamorgan Railway where they were normally attached to sets of two close coupled coaches comprising a four-wheeled 1888 composite coach and a six-wheeled 1895 brake third known as 'Motor Sets'.

The sole survivor of former Barry Railway Class E 0-6-0T No. 784 is seen in this undated view at Barry its home shed. *Neville Stead*

Scottish Floods Update

UPDATE ON SCOTTISH FLOOD BRIDGE RECONSTRUCTION

Following the disastrous floods of August 1948 which breached the ECML in numerous places, as reported in the last issue, progress has been made in replacing the temporary structures, which allowed the line to be re-opened within 3 months, with more permanent works. The following views were all taken on 17 March 1949 and show how much had been achieved in a short space of time at four locations and similarly what still remained to be done.

Top - Bridge No. 123.

Bottom - Bridge No. 125.

Top - Bridge No. 130 from the west.

Right - 17 March 1949. Bridge No. 133 South buttresses from west showing timber shuttering.

All images courtesy of Lorne Anton / Ayton Local History Society.

Ship Ahoy!

Since nationalisation seven new ships have been brought into service on BR routes to the Isle of Wight, Ireland and the Continent. The latest is *MV Hibernia* the first of two twin screw 5,000 hp motor passenger vessels ordered by the LMR from Harland & Wolff and launched in April 1948. She set sail from Holyhead at 5:45am on 14 April on her first trip to Kingstown (Dun Laoghaire). Together with her sister ship, the *MV Cambria*, she served on the Irish route for many years. Carrying 2,000 passengers there were berths and cabins for 436 in First and Third class accommodation. Dining facilities are provided on a particularly generous scale.

In view of the often rough nature of the Irish Sea crossing, in 1951 she was fitted with Denny-Brown stabilisers. In 1964-65 the vessel was refurbished with airline style seating with some cabins and staterooms being removed and replaced with Second class lounges and a cafeteria. The First and Second class smoke rooms were converted into a tea lounge. In 1976 she was sold to the Agapitos Brothers in Greece being renamed the *Express Apollon* but she never traded in Greece. She remained laid up at Salamina until sold to a firm of Indian breakers, Ankom Solid Steel Traders, in 1980 being subsequently scrapped.

On 4 April this year some 150 BR ships, including those sailing from the Channel ports to the Continent and the Channel Islands, from the Humber ports to the Continent, from North West ports to Ireland, on Clyde and Loch Lomond steamers and on Plymouth tenders and ferries, hoisted a new house flag which will also be flown by BR's marine shore establishments.

In addition to the *MV Hibernia* there are vessels under construction at the present time destined for the Newhaven – Dieppe service and for the Harwich – Hook of Holland route. Next year a new Harwich – Zeebrugge train ferry and a Portsmouth – Isle of Wight ferry are expected to be delivered. Delivery in 1952 is anticipated for a new Channel Islands vessel currently on order.

MV Hibernia recorded at Holyhead. *Sydney Roberts*

Also making the news

British Railway's first year of operation revealed income of £337m against expenses of £311m leading to gross receipts of £26m. *(Ed: BR would remain profitable until 1956 after which large losses were incurred.)*

"Cambridge & Garden Cities Buffet Car Express' reinstated after suspension during WW2.

Resumption of locomotive building at Gorton works with 10 class B1's.

Contract let for new tunnel at Woodhead.

New numbering system for motive power depots 1-29 LMR, 30-39 ER (Eastern Section), 40-49 ER (Western Section), 50-59 NER, 60-69 ScR, 70-79 SR, 80-99 WR.

Gas turbine No. 18100 undergoing trials in Switzerland.

Last of the big four companies dissolved.

Bo-peep tunnel near St. Leonards closed for repairs.

A locomotive naming committee was formed in March 1949 consisting of D S M Barrie, Railway Executive Public Relations Officer, E S Cox, British Railways Executive Officer design and Geoge Dow, Public Relations and Publicity Officer BR London Midland Region. At first none of the standard classes were going to be named but a public outcry forced a change of policy and the railway executive has stated officially that "...there is no intention of removing the existing names on locomotives or of discontinuing the general practice of naming locomotives in suitable cases."

Thirteen more named trains introduced including two re-introductions one of which was 'The Fenman'.

Following the appalling accident statistics from 1948, during which there were 60 fatalities and 238 serious injuries, it is pleasing to announce that no passengers were killed in train accidents on BR during 1949, a record not equalled since 1908. However, this was no cause for complacency for this statement needs to be read in the context that there were still 12 train accidents that resulted in fatalities to persons other than passengers and that 44 passengers were killed

Ex GER Class D16/3 No.62606 leaves Kings Lynn with the up 'Fenman'. This 4-4-0 was based at Kings Lynn shed from 1953 until withdrawal in September 1959. This variant of the class was introduced in 1936 being a rebuild of the D15 type with a larger boiler, round topped firebox, modified footplating and 9½" piston valves. From its introduction until the end of steam haulage in 1959 the 6:50 am train from Hunstanton to London Liverpool Street and the return working, leaving Liverpool Street at 4:40 pm, was named 'The Fenman'. After that date the service was truncated to commence from King's Lynn. *Harry Cartright*

In this current year of 2023 which has seen the first coronation for 70 years it is perhaps appropriate to include a view of the coaches of that other 'Coronation', the express service introduced by the LNER in July 1937 to mark the coronation of George V1 and Queen Elizabeth. Coaches of the down train are seen here but now relegated for use in an ordinary service recorded at Holloway in 1949.
Roy Vincent

in movement accidents as opposed to train accidents, the principal causes being misadventure or carelessness on the part of the passengers themselves. Deaths and injuries to railway staff were still by today's standards very high at 188 and 2625 respectively. An example of the fatalities still being incurred is the accident that occurred at Oakley on the London Midland Region on 4 October 1949. The 1.35 pm. freight train proceeding from Wellingborough to Brent and travelling on the up goods line under clear signals collided at about 30 mph with the rear of the 12.40 pm freight train, also proceeding from Wellingborough to Brent, the brakevan of which was standing on Oakley viaduct near mile post 531. The engine and 14 loaded coal wagons of the 1.35 pm train plunged over the viaduct and came to rest on the bank of the River Ouse 25 ft. below. The driver and fireman were killed instantly. The brakevan and five wagons of the 12.40 pm train were derailed with the wreckage piling up on the down goods line.

Although the ½ mile steeply graded spur connection between the West Highland route and the Callander & Oban route at Crianlarich was brought into use as far back as 1894 it has previously only been used by freight trains and occasional excursions. With the introduction of the summer timetable on 23 May 1949 one passenger service in each direction between Glasgow Queen Street (High level) and Oban is now using this spur thus reducing the distance between Glasgow and Oban by some 16 miles compared to the C&O route via Stirling and Callander. Black 5 No. 45357 is seen here in 1961 with a freight service from the C&O's Crianlarich Lower station crossing over the junction with the spur line on the right which leads up to the West Highland's Upper station.
Transport Library

The Up marshalling yard at Cambridgeshire's Whitemoor facility has been selected for a trial of radio telephony as part of the Railway Executive's programme to examine the feasibility of the application of radio to engineering and traffic operations. The control tower has been provided with a fixed radio transmitter with remote control in the foreman's cabin, and mobile equipment has been installed in the first of four diesel electric shunting locomotives used in the yard. It is hoped to reduce the amount of time taken in passing instructions from ground control staff to locomotive drivers and will hopefully provide an easier means of communication when adverse weather conditions such as fog and snow prevail. Transmissions are normally conducted between the foreman's hump-cabin and the shunter locomotive crew but staff in control of the numerous points in the yard have the facility to interrupt and speak directly to drivers in case of emergency.

A video dating from 1951 is available on Youtube and it is claimed in the commentary that radio control "saves hours a day of expensive engine time" and messages can be seen and heard being passed from the Control Tower to one of the shunters designated "Shunt Able" where for the benefit of the cameras the message is "Received and understood. Over". Another instruction, this time to "Shunt Baker" is for him to speed up from 1½ mph to 2mph in order to get a rake of seven wagons over the hump.

Left - Whitemoor marshalling yard photographed looking down the hump.
Transport Library

Below - A wagon on the retarders of the Up hump. *Transport Library*

Amongst the items it is intended to feature the following –

New Regional Boundaries

7000th. Locomotive built at Crewe

Gas turbine No. 18000

WR 16xx class Pannier Tank

Southampton Ocean Terminal opened

New Red Dragon express

The last Ivatt Atlantic

Final days of the Sheppey Light Railway

'Fell' locomotive No. 10100